D1359619

ALETHEIA Paperbacks now available
for your individual or group study:

An Adventure in Love
  W. Taliaferro Thompson
Adventures in Parenthood
  W. Taliaferro Thompson
The Bible in Christian Teaching
  Holmes Rolston
A Call to Faith
  Rachel Henderlite
The Creative Era
  Carl G. Howie
The Enduring Message of the Bible
  L. Harold DeWolf
Faces about the Christ
  Holmes Rolston
Forgiveness and Hope
  Rachel Henderlite
The Gospel According to Mark and Its Meaning for Today
  Ernest Trice Thompson
Handbook for Christian Believers
  A. J. Ungersma
In the Beginning God
  William M. Logan
The Nature and Mission of the Church
  Donald G. Miller
Out of the Whirlwind
  William B. Ward
Reasons for Our Faith
  Henry T. Close
The Revelation of Jesus Christ
  Donald W. Richardson
Scripture and the Christian Response
  Howard Tillman Kuist
The Sermon on the Mount and Its Meaning for Today
  Ernest Trice Thompson
The Story of the Reformation
  William Stevenson
Understanding the Books of the New Testament
  edited by Patrick H. Carmichael
Understanding the Books of the Old Testament
  edited by Patrick H. Carmichael
We Believe
  Henry Wade DuBose

FACES ABOUT THE CHRIST

Faces

ZACHARIAS • ELISABETH

MARY • JOSEPH

SIMEON • ANNA

HEROD THE GREAT

JOHN THE BAPTIST

NICODEMUS

A WOMAN OF SAMARIA

SIMON • ZACCHAEUS

A CENTURION FROM CAPERNAUM

THE SAMARITAN WHO GAVE THANKS

THE RICH YOUNG RULER • SALOME

MARTHA • MARY OF BETHANY • LAZARUS

by Holmes Rolston

about the Christ

SIMON PETER · ANDREW · JAMES · JOHN

PHILIP · NATHANAEL

ANNAS · CAIAPHAS

THOMAS · MATTHEW

PONTIUS PILATE

JAMES THE SON OF ALPHAEUS

HEROD ANTIPAS

JUDAS, NOT ISCARIOT

BARABBAS · SIMON OF CYRENE

SIMON THE ZEALOT

THE THIEF ON THE CROSS

JUDAS ISCARIOT

THE CENTURION AT THE CROSS

JOSEPH OF ARIMATHAEA · MARY MAGDALENE · CLEOPAS

THE FACE OF THE CHRIST

John Knox Press
Richmond, Virginia

Library of Congress Catalog Card Number: 58-9909

Aletheia edition 1966

Unless otherwise indicated, Scripture quotations are from the King James Version. Those from the *Revised Standard Version of the Bible* are copyrighted 1946 and 1952.

Copyright © 1959 by C. D. Deans, Richmond, Virginia
Aletheia edition © M. E. Bratcher 1966

Printed in the United States of America

J. 4066

To my children, Holmes III, Mary Jacqueline, and Julia Long, companions with me in seeking the face of the Christ.

ACKNOWLEDGMENTS

I wish to thank Rev. J. J. Murray of Lexington, Virginia, Rev. Hunter B. Blakely of the Presbyterian Board of Christian Education, and the editorial staff of John Knox Press for the invaluable aid which they have given in the preparation of the manuscript of this book.

Contents

FACES OF THE TWELVE

FACES OF THE PASSION WEEK

THE FACE OF THE CHRIST

Prologue

The men and women whom we meet in our study of the four Gospels are of interest to us because of their association with Jesus. They are an intensely human group of people who have been rescued from oblivion by the fact that they came into contact with Jesus of Nazareth. They are important to us because we see the face of the Christ as we study the faces of those who gather about Him. We are interested in hearing what Jesus said to the men and women of His own generation in order that we may have some understanding of what He would say to us as we face the human problems of our time. We want to know His contemporaries' reaction to Jesus so that we may find help in understanding people's responses to Him today.

The starting point of any study of the personalities around Jesus must be found in the Gospels. This is our starting point. The actual beginning was the appearance in history of the Person to whom the Gospels point. Jesus made His impact on His own generation. He gathered around Him a group of followers who became known as His disciples. He aroused also the opposition of the religious leaders of His time. They put Him to death. The New Testament Church was called into being through the witness of His followers to His resurrection. Jesus created the believing community which has given us the New Testament. The four Gospels are part of the witness of the Church to her Lord. First there was the revelation event. Second there was the believing community. And third there was the written record through which this community gave an account of itself to the world.

As we study in detail the Biblical material which throws light

on the characters of the friends and foes of Jesus we find that
we must go to the Fourth Gospel for much of our source material.
We realize that this Gospel is written from a somewhat different
point of view from that of the first three Gospels and that it contains interpretations as well as history. We do feel, however, that
in its study of the characters of the Gospels it is dependable as
history.

These studies of the faces about the Christ are based on the assumption that the figure of Jesus which meets us in the four Gospels is essentially in harmony with the Jesus who actually lived
and suffered and died—and rose from the dead—in Palestine in
the years 4 B.C.—A.D. 30. The New Testament Church did not
create the Jesus of the Gospels. Instead the Jesus whom we meet
in the Gospels is the One who called the New Testament Church
into existence. We do not deny the historicity of Jesus when we
say that the Gospels which point to Him have come from the
believing community. Every great event of history is best understood as it is seen in perspective by those who have understood
its real significance.

There is mystery here because the One to whom the Gospels
point is a unique Person, a divine-human Person who meets us
in the context of our earthly life. If we assume that such a Person
could never have existed, we have prejudged our case before we
start. The fatal flaw in some of the critical approaches to the
Gospels is that they have been based on the assumption that such
a Person as the Jesus who is pictured in the Gospels could never
have existed. But on such an assumption we cannot explain the
existence of the believing fellowship of the New Testament, and
we can give no adequate account of the origin of the Gospels.
All attempts to explain the New Testament on the basis of a
Jesus of history who would fit without offense into the patterns
of modern thought have broken down. But if we admit that the
Gospels give us a true picture of the Jesus who actually lived, we
are immediately set in the place of decision and judgment. We
cannot remain indifferent to the Jesus who comes to us in the

New Testament. The writer of the Fourth Gospel can say of Him: "In the beginning was the Word, and the Word was with God, and the Word was God. . . . And the Word was made flesh, and dwelt among us, (and we beheld his glory, the glory as of the only begotten of the Father,) full of grace and truth." (John 1:1, 14.) This is mystery. It is the infinite mystery of the Incarnation in which God is manifest in the flesh. But it is mystery which has a shining light at its center. Jesus said of Himself: "I am the light of the world: he that followeth me shall not walk in darkness, but shall have the light of life." (John 8:12.)

This book contains a series of character studies of the personalities around Jesus. These pictures of the faces about the Christ are based upon the Gospel records. They are an effort to express in terms that are meaningful to life today the things that Jesus said to the people who gathered around Him. A few of these characters are known to us in secular history. This is true particularly of those who were opposed to Jesus, such as the Herods and Pilate, or Caiaphas and Annas. But most of these characters are known to us only through their appearance in the Gospel narratives.

As we study the various individuals who appear in the Gospel narratives we find that in many cases we are confined by the limited nature of our sources. Often we have only one or two brief references. We have resisted the temptation to create imaginary incidents. Instead we have sought to center attention on a question asked of Jesus or on something that Jesus has said which gives a clue to us as we seek to know His mind in the decisions we have to make today.

We face a different dilemma as we study the major characters of the Gospels. Here we are embarrassed by the richness of our material. Within the limits of one chapter we cannot deal adequately with all of the stories which have been preserved for us. It is possible, for example, to write a whole series of thirteen Sunday school lessons on the life of Peter. It has not seemed wise, however, to alter our pattern and give several chapters to some individuals. We have sought rather to give briefly the significance of the character as a whole and then to concentrate on one important incident. The reader will understand that this procedure gives a picture that is obviously out of proportion. A book which gives as much space to Judas, not Iscariot, as to John the Baptist is not true to the emphasis of the New Testament; but such a book can be faithful to its purpose of presenting Jesus in His relation to His contemporaries.

In a similar study of the personalities around Paul, the writer limited himself to a study of the characters known to us by name. But the importance of some of the unnamed characters of the Gospels has made advisable the inclusion of a few characters such as the woman of Samaria. No attempt has been made to give an exhaustive study of all of these characters.

A peculiar difficulty faces the writer who attempts to describe the characters who stand around Jesus. We can analyze their human predicaments and seek to understand the message of Jesus to them. We can study their reactions to the demands which Jesus makes on them. But it is difficult to deal with the impact of the people around Him on Jesus Himself. He had a great capacity for friendship. He called His disciples *His friends* and made known to them the things which He had received from His Father. He loved people like Mary and Martha and Lazarus and the beloved disciple. He spoke with appreciation of the way in which the disciples continued with Him in His temptations. (Luke 22:28.) He loved people and was loved by them.

We know that Jesus was moved by compassion and by righteous indignation. But we cannot go behind the record and seek to analyze His motives or enter into His thought processes. We can understand the witness of Jesus to Himself. We can listen with interest to the disclosure of Himself which Jesus makes to individuals in the New Testament. But we cannot describe the extent to which John or Peter influenced Jesus. Jesus moves and acts out of an inner assurance which we cannot hope to fully comprehend. It is comparatively simple to show the way in which Paul was influenced by other people, but we are baffled when we try to deal in a similar way with Jesus. Perhaps this is one aspect of that uniqueness of the Person of Jesus which always amazes us.

In our effort to deal with the various personalities of the Gospels we cannot escape certain conclusions concerning Jesus Himself. If the Gospels are to be understood at all, they must be understood in the light of the central fact to which they point. If God was in Christ reconciling the world unto Himself, the Gospels make sense. And they cannot be understood apart from that acknowledgment of Jesus as Lord which is their central theme. When we study the life of Paul, we are dealing with a character in history who is significant for us today because of the Christ to whom he points. But when we deal with the Jesus of the Gospels we are coming into contact with One who was a definite Person in history and is at the same time the Eternal Contemporary of every age and every civilization. The basic assumption of the Christian Church is that Jesus of Nazareth is also the risen Lord seated at the right hand of God in glory and in power, and present with His Church.

This understanding of the Church as to *who Jesus is* gives eternal significance to the things that He said and did in the days of His flesh. The conviction of the Church is that we have here a key to the mind and heart of God. This Jesus who meets us in the pages of the New Testament comes to each of us as our personal Saviour from sin. He comes also as our Judge and as the Judge of our society. He forces us to decide for Him or against Him. And this decision is crucial for our eternal destiny. As John puts it: "He that believeth on the Son hath everlasting life: and he that believeth not the Son shall not see life; but the wrath of God abideth on him." (John 3:36.) We are interested in the men and women of the New Testament because through a study of what Jesus said to them we may prepare the way for His confrontation of men and women today.

Faces About the Manger

"A certain priest named Zacharias ... righteous before God, walking in all the commandments and ordinances of the Lord blameless."—Luke 1:5-6.

1. ZACHARIAS

Scripture background: Luke 1:5-25, 39-80.

The New Testament narrative of the events connected with Jesus' birth begins with the message to Zacharias, the father of John the Baptist. The real beginning is with God. It is not for us to know the times or the seasons which the Father has put in His own power. But we can know that in the wisdom of God the time had come for Him to send His Son into the world. The message to Zacharias is the first of those acts of God by which the human actors in the great drama of redemption are called upon to co-operate with the purposes of God.

The angel Gabriel comes to Zacharias and to Mary. God speaks through dreams to Joseph. The voice of prophecy, long silent in Israel, reawakens with Zacharias and Mary, with Simeon and Anna, who speak in the first hymns of the Nativity. Fear falls on the heart of Herod the Great. Shepherds worship at the manger. Magi come from the distant East in search of the King of the Jews. Mary alone of the faces about the manger is to be found with Jesus in the days of His public ministry. The personalities of the Nativity, therefore, do not experience a genuine confrontation with our Lord in His ministry of preaching and teaching. But the study of them does create an atmosphere of expectancy. We stand here in the anteroom to the throne. We have time to lose the glare of the street and to be prepared for the vision of the King.

Zacharias was a priest of the division of Abijah. His wife was of the daughters of Aaron and her name was Elisabeth. This man and his wife represented the best of the piety of Israel. Luke tells us that they were "righteous before God, walking in all the commandments and ordinances of the Lord blameless." (Luke 1:6.) This does not mean that they were perfect. Zacharias is slow to believe the word which comes to him. Zacharias and his wife were childless; they had hoped and prayed for the child that never came. When Elisabeth passed the normal age for the bearing of children their hope grew dim, but their yearning for a child of their own was as strong as ever.

Luke tells us that the event which he is about to describe took place in the days of Herod, king of Judea. We are dealing here not with a myth but with an event. It happens to a man named Zacharias, in the sanctuary of the Temple toward the close of the reign of Herod the king. The reference is, of course, to Herod the Great. It gives in part the setting for the story. When Zacharias enters the Temple he belongs to a conquered people ruled over by a king—an evil king descended from the rulers of Edom and supported in his power by the armies of Rome. It is not difficult to understand the yearning of Zacharias for the deliverance of his people from the hands of their enemies.

We do not need to follow in detail the story which Luke unfolds in his first chapter. We should notice that Gabriel comes also to Mary, and that the sign to Mary of the truth of his words is the fulfillment of the promise to Zacharias and Elisabeth. We should remember that Mary goes at once to the home of Elisabeth and stays there until shortly before the birth of John the Baptist. It is in the light of the information which he must have received from Mary that Zacharias speaks the great prophecy found in Luke 1: 68-79. These words are uttered under the inspiration of the Holy Spirit. The aged priest rejoices in the birth of his son and moves on to the greater hope of the birth of the Son of God. He is aware of the special function which John is to perform. But he is thinking also of the full redemption which is involved when God comes to us in Jesus Christ.

Zacharias says that God in the sending of His Son is acting decisively for the redemption of His people. The God of Israel is the God who reveals Himself in His mighty deeds. In the Incarnation, God enters our human life for the salvation of His people. Zacharias is sure, too, that God acts in fulfillment of His covenant relation to Israel. God moves to fulfill the word which "he spake by the mouth of his holy prophets, which have been since the world began." (Luke 1:70.) He seeks "to perform the mercy promised to our fathers, and to remember his holy covenant; the oath which he sware to our father Abraham." (Luke 1:72-73.) The New Testament writers all agree that the coming of Jesus is in fulfillment of the covenant. Zacharias is a link between the believing past and the believing community of the New Testament.

It is not surprising that Zacharias expresses the hope for the deliverance of his people from political bondage. He hopes that the birth of the Christ will mean "that we should be saved from our enemies, and from the hand of all that hate us." (Luke 1:71.) He gives classic expression to this hope when he prays that God "would grant unto us, that we being delivered out of the hand of our enemies might serve him without fear, in holiness and righteousness before him, all the days of our life." (Luke 1:74-75.) The desire for freedom is properly expressed here. Zacharias does not ask for freedom from tyranny in order that he may do as he pleases. He seeks deliverance from oppression in order that he and his people may be free to serve the Lord without fear. He seeks to walk before the Lord in holiness and righteousness all his days. Here again he has expressed the yearning of many people today. Christians who are living in lands where the Church is persecuted seek most of all the freedom of worship. They want freedom to worship God without fear according to the dictates of their own conscience. There is a sense in which the hope of Zacharias was cruelly disappointed. Jesus was rejected by His own people and crucified by the Romans. The son of Zacharias spent his last days in Herod's prison and was executed by command of the tyrant; the Son of Mary did not deliver him. In less than a century the Jewish state ceased to exist. But there is a deeper sense in which his words are true. When men have acknowledged Jesus as Lord they have found the power to stand against the tyrannies of earth. Someone has said that men will either be ruled by God or they will be ruled by tyrants. It is also true that the men who know that they must obey God rather than man will not permanently submit to tyranny. When men have genuinely sought the freedom to serve God without fear they have laid the foundations of both political and religious freedom. But these freedoms root in the deeper salvation which Zacharias goes on to proclaim.

In verses 77-79 Zacharias analyzes the salvation which John is to proclaim. There is no attempt here to distinguish between the work of John and Jesus. Zacharias is giving the significance for all mankind of that salvation which God has begun to proclaim in the birth of the prophet who is to prepare the way for Jesus. This salvation contains at least three elements. It is first of all a proclamation of the remission of sins to those who receive it. The New Testament writers never forget that the fundamental flaw in human life is man's rebellion against God—man's sin and man's alienation from God through his sin, and man's slavery to his own lusts. In the events which are to take place Zacharias sees an expression of the tender mercy of God in which He comes to man to proclaim the forgiveness of sins. Zacharias knows that God in Christ is reconciling the world unto Himself. As he thinks of the mercy of God in Christ, he likens it to the coming of dawn to a darkened world. And this figure of speech leads him to his second great affirmation. He says that God in Christ has acted "to give light to them that sit in darkness and in the shadow of death." We think here of the words of Jesus when He said: "I am the light of the world: he that followeth me shall not walk in darkness, but shall have the light of life." (John 8:12.) This is a salvation which gives light to those who sit in the shadow of death. If there be a salvation it must be one which penetrates the ultimate mystery of human death.

Zacharias says also that God has moved "to guide our feet into the way of peace." The immediate reference here may be to the peace with God which comes when men receive the reconciliation God has wrought out in Jesus Christ. But Zacharias speaks with a keen sense of the political situation. He is hoping for One who can guide his people in the way of peace. Here again the immediate hope was not realized. Jesus did not guide the Jewish nation into the way of peace. Instead the nation which had rejected its Messiah perished in a futile war with Rome. But we have not forgotten the words of Zacharias. We live in a world which is threatened with atomic destruction. Our generation needs desperately someone to "guide our feet into the way of peace." If we are to find peace today we must learn from Jesus. We must learn to seek justice. We must learn to forgive our enemies. We must learn to love them. We must learn to seek the good for them. If we follow Jesus in the way of justice and love we will find that He is guiding our feet into the way of peace.

The son of Zacharias was to go before the Christ to prepare the people for His coming so that He might bring to them and to all mankind the forgiveness of sins, the light of the Gospel, and the insights which lead to peace.

"Blessed is she who believed that there would be a fulfillment of what was spoken to her from the Lord."— Luke 1:45, Revised Standard Version.

2. ELISABETH

Scripture background: Luke 1:5-80.

Elisabeth was childless. She had passed the age at which women normally give birth to children. She refers to this when she says: "Thus the Lord has done to me in the days when he looked on me, to take away my reproach among men." (Luke 1:25, R.S.V.) The experience of motherhood had not been granted to Elisabeth, and she felt keenly that she had missed one of woman's supreme experiences. The modern woman has an opportunity for a career, which was not possible to Elisabeth. When childlessness is part of the providential discipline of God, it can be borne creatively. Many women to whom God has not given children have ministered in the name of the Lord to the children of their community. But the yearning of woman for the experience of motherhood still remains basic to human life.

We can imagine that when Zacharias reached home after his experience in the Temple, Elisabeth was at first concerned about her husband's loss of the power of speech. We can also be sure that Zacharias did not lose much time in communicating to her through writing the story of the visit of Gabriel and the promise that a child was to be born to them in their old age. We do not know the reaction of Elisabeth to this news. In a similar situation Sarah, the wife of Abraham, expressed her incredulity in laughter. (Genesis 18:12.) Zacharias had been slow to believe the word of the angel, and it is possible that Elisabeth also had her struggle between faith and unbelief. She may speak out of her own experience of struggle with doubt when she says to Mary: "Blessed is she who believed that there would be a fulfillment of what was spoken to her from the Lord." (Luke 1:45, R.S.V.) Elisabeth stopped going out and hid herself from the eyes of others as she waited for the fulfillment of the word of the Lord.

Six months after his appearance to Zacharias in the Temple, the angel Gabriel, the most exalted of heaven's messengers, was sent again to earth. He came to Nazareth, a city of Galilee, to a virgin betrothed to a man named Joseph, of the house of David. The virgin's name was Mary. Gabriel announces to Mary the divine decision that she has been chosen to be the mother of the Christ. After he has made his announcement Gabriel gives Mary a sign. He says: "And behold, Elisabeth thy kinswoman, she also hath conceived a son in her old age; and this is the sixth month with her that was called barren. For no word from God shall be void of power." (Luke 1:36-37, American Standard Version.) The angel is not saying that God can do the thing which is self-contradictory. He is saying that God can and will keep His promises. God has the power to accomplish His word.

When the angel tells Mary that it is now the sixth month with her cousin Elisabeth, who was called barren, Mary believes the word spoken to her and accepts her place in the divine purpose. She says: "Behold I am the handmaid of the Lord; let it be to me according to your word." (Luke 1:38, R.S.V.) When she has said this the angel departs from her.

After the angel had vanished, "Mary arose . . . and went into the hill country with haste, into a city of Judah; and entered into the house of Zacharias and saluted Elisabeth." (Luke 1:39-40, A.S.V.) It is not difficult to imagine the conflicting emotions Mary experienced as she made this journey, which must have taken her several days, from Nazareth of Galilee to the home of Zacharias in the hill country of Judea. The angel had vanished from her sight. Her memory of the experience was sharp and clear, but she must have wondered if she had been the victim of a hallucination. Could it be that she, a virgin, was to give birth to the One who was to be the Messiah of her people? There was one visible sign to which Mary could turn. The angel had told her of her cousin Elisabeth's condition. If this sign was verified, Mary would have a firm faith for the days ahead. If, on the contrary, she should find that nothing had happened to Elisabeth, she would feel that she must have been the victim of a delusion.

It is in the midst of this struggle between doubt and faith that Mary crosses the threshold of the home of Zacharias and calls to Elisabeth. And as Mary stands before her, Elisabeth knows through the Holy Spirit that she is in the presence of the woman who is to be the mother of the long-expected Messiah. Speaking under the inspiration of the Holy Spirit, Elisabeth says to Mary: "Blessed are you among women, and blessed is the fruit of your womb! And why is this granted me, that the mother of my Lord should come to me? For behold, when the voice of your greeting came to my ears, the babe in my womb leaped for joy. And blessed is she who believed that there would be a fulfillment of what was spoken to her from the Lord." (Luke 1:42-45, R.S.V.)

The words of Elisabeth give Mary the assurance she desperately needs. It is in reply to Elisabeth that she speaks the Magnificat. However, our central concern at this time is not with the words

of Mary but with Elisabeth's message to Mary. The thought of
Elisabeth is not with herself or even with her son. She refers to
herself only to say that she is not worthy of this visit. She makes
no reference to the future of her son. The center of her interest
is with the Son of Mary and with the faith of Mary. She faces
Mary and says: "And why is this granted me, that the mother
of my Lord should come to me?" Elisabeth was probably the
first person to acknowledge Mary's Son as her Lord. In this she
anticipates the message of the angel who on the night of the
Nativity announces to the shepherds: "To you is born this day
in the city of David a Savior, who is Christ the Lord." (Luke
2:11, R.S.V.)

Elisabeth calls attention to Mary's faith as she says, "Blessed is
she who believed that there would be a fulfillment of what was
spoken to her from the Lord." (Luke 1:45, R.S.V.) The faith
of Mary which Elisabeth describes here is similar to the faith
Abraham revealed in his belief that God would give him a son in
his old age. Concerning Abraham, Paul writes: "And being not
weak in faith, he considered not his own body now dead, when
he was about an hundred years old, neither yet the deadness of
Sarah's womb: he staggered not at the promise of God through
unbelief; but was strong in faith, giving glory to God; and being
fully persuaded that, what he had promised, he was able also to
perform. And therefore it was imputed to him for righteousness.
Now it was not written for his sake alone, that it was imputed
to him; but for us also, to whom it shall be imputed, if we believe
on him that raised up Jesus our Lord from the dead; who was delivered for our offences, and was raised again for our justification." (Romans 4:19-25.)

The common element in the faith of Abraham, the faith of
Elisabeth, and the faith of Mary was that each in his own situation believed that what God had promised He was able to perform. Through this faith each of these found acceptance with
God.

Paul moves at once from this example of faith to the full faith
of the believing Christian. The Christian knows that God will

be and will do to him as He has promised in His Word. When we believe that God can and will keep the promises He has made in His Word, God accepts us as righteous in His sight.

Paul in Galatians uses the language of birth to describe the experience in which the Christ comes to live in the human heart. He writes: "My little children, of whom I travail in birth again until Christ be formed in you." (Galatians 4:19.) The mystery of the Incarnation must be followed by the mystery of the indwelling Christ.

> Though Christ a thousand times
> In Bethlehem be born,
> If He is not born in thee
> Thy soul is still forlorn.*

When a man believes that God in Christ has forgiven his sins and set him in a new relation to Himself, he comes into this vital union with Christ.

It is in writing to the Colossians that Paul uses the expression, "Christ in you, the hope of glory." (Colossians 1:27.) The Christian's hope of glory is rooted in the promises which God has made in His Word. The Christian's hope of ultimate entrance into the glory of heaven is in seeming contradiction to the reign of sin and death over our entire human existence. But here again the Christian believes that the word spoken unto him from the Lord will be fulfilled. He is able to face the end of his earthly existence in the certainty that no word from God shall be void of power and in the confidence that the God who brought again from the dead our Lord Jesus Christ is both able and willing to keep His promises. The faith which Elisabeth saw in Mary points the way to both justification and glorification.

* Angelus Silesius, "In Thine Own Heart," *Masterpieces of Religious Verse*, p. 148. New York: Harper & Brothers, 1948. By permission.

"Behold the handmaid of the Lord . . ."—Luke 1:38.

3. MARY

Scripture background: Luke 1:26—2:52; Mark 3:31-35; Matthew 12:46-50; Luke 8:19-21; John 2:1-5; 19:25-27; Acts 1:14; Galatians 4:4.

"Born of woman" must mean born of *a* woman. There is nothing more intensely personal than birth. We cannot enter into the divine decision in which one woman was selected to be the mother of the Christ. But we know that when the time had come for God to send His Son into the world it became necessary to announce to this woman the destiny that was to be hers. The angel Gabriel, who had already been sent to Zacharias, was the bearer of God's message to Mary. (Luke 1:26-27.)

We do not know the form in which the angel appeared. He may have spoken in a dream. He may have appeared to her as a man. We do know that Gabriel "came in unto" Mary and said, "Hail, thou that art highly favoured, the Lord is with thee: blessed art thou among women." Mary is troubled at this saying. She does not understand the meaning of the words she has heard.

Gabriel continues: "Do not be afraid, Mary, for you have found favor with God. And behold, you will conceive in your womb and bear a son, and you shall call his name Jesus. He will be great, and will be called the Son of the Most High; and the Lord God will give to him the throne of his father David, and he will reign over the house of Jacob for ever; and of his kingdom there will be no end." (Luke 1:30-33, R.S.V.) Mary's answer is the one any woman would have made in a similar situation. She says simply, "How can this be, since I have no husband?" (Luke 1:34, R.S.V.) The angel replies: "The Holy Spirit will come upon you, and the power of the Most High will overshadow you; therefore the child to be born will be called holy, the Son of God." (Luke 1:35, R.S.V.)

Having announced the miraculous birth of Jesus, Gabriel gives

Mary a sign. The sign of the truth of his words is that her cousin Elisabeth, who is far beyond the normal age for childbearing, is to give birth to a son and is now in her sixth month. John's birth is supernatural in that his conception comes when his mother has passed the time for bearing children. The birth of Jesus is supernatural in that He is born of a virgin. Having made his statements concerning both Elisabeth and Mary, the angel gives a cause adequate to produce these exceptions to the course of nature. He says: "For no word from God shall be void of power." (Luke 1:37, A.S.V.) God's word is God's decision. God's word is also God's act. He is able to accomplish His will. That which He promises He is able also to perform.

Mary believes the word spoken to her. She says: "Behold I am the handmaid of the Lord; let it be to me according to your word." (Luke 1:38, R.S.V.) She accepts the divine destiny and co-operates voluntarily with God's purpose for her. The angel departs and Mary is left alone.

We do not need to follow the details of the familiar story of Jesus' birth in Bethlehem. We do need to notice that when the shepherds make known the saying which had been told them concerning the child, "Mary kept all these things, pondering them in her heart." (Luke 2:19, R.S.V.) When Simeon a little later makes his announcement concerning the baby Jesus, it is said that "his mother marveled at what was said about him." (Luke 2:33, R.S.V.) Mary knew she was the instrument of a divine purpose, but she knew also that there were many things about this Son of hers which she would never fully understand.

After the flight into Egypt and a brief sojourn there, Joseph and Mary returned with Jesus to Nazareth. Here Mary lived the life of a wife and mother. The simple and obvious interpretation of the New Testament narrative is that Mary as the wife of Joseph gave birth to sons and daughters. When Jesus visits Nazareth in His public ministry, the people say: "Is not this the carpenter, the son of Mary, the brother of James, and Joses, and of Juda, and Simon? and are not his sisters here with us?" (Mark 6:3. See also Matthew 13:55-56.) We have no finer tribute to the purity and holiness of the marriage relation than the fact that

God willed for the woman who gave birth to Jesus to be also the mother of other sons and daughters.

We have a brief glimpse of Mary in connection with the visit of Jesus to the Temple at the age of twelve. There is a gentle rebuke to her in Jesus' words as He says: "How is it that ye sought me? Wist ye not that I must be about my Father's business?" (Luke 2:49.) The story is recorded because it reveals the knowledge which the boy of twelve had of His peculiar relation with the Father in heaven and also His feeling that Joseph and Mary should have understood this. Here again we realize that Mary could not fully understand her Son.

The years of Jesus' public ministry were probably for Mary a time of alternating faith and doubt. She takes the initiative in turning to Jesus when the wine fails in the wedding feast at Cana. Jesus replies that His hour is not yet come; but, following His mother's suggestion, He reveals His power by turning the water into wine. At this time His disciples first became conscious of His supernatural powers. (John 2:1-11.) But a little later His mother and brethren come to Jesus in the midst of His ministry in Galilee with the probable intention of persuading Him to give up His work. It is in this connection that Jesus disparages the physical tie between Him and His mother and brethren and emphasizes His spiritual kinship with all those who choose to do the will of God. (Mark 3:31-35.) We need to remember this when we are tempted to exalt Mary unduly.

The most difficult burden Mary had to bear must have been the rapid growth of opposition to Jesus. She may have been in the synagogue at Nazareth when the people with whom she and her sons had lived for many years sought to put Jesus to death. Simeon had told her that her Son would be a sign which would be spoken against. He had said also that a sword would pierce through her own soul. Mary came to know that the experience of being the mother of the Christ did not mean immunity from suffering. In and through her own Son, she knew the capacity of a mother for suffering. The full depths were sounded as she stood in the presence of her crucified Son and knew that life had departed from His body. The deepest element in Mary's sorrow

was not the suffering which comes to a mother who must see her
son suffer and die. When she passed through the experience of
Calvary, Mary must have known the despair of one who feels
that the promises of God have failed. She who had heard the
words of Gabriel concerning His birth now beheld her Son lifeless on the cross.

Mary's dilemma was not resolved until the morning of the
Resurrection. Then she knew the meaning of the promise that
her Son should reign over the house of Jacob forever and that
of His Kingdom there should be no end. The last picture of Mary
in the New Testament is when, with her sons around her, she
meets for prayer with those who on Mount Olivet have seen
the risen Lord ascended to the glory of His Father in heaven.
(Acts 1:14.)

There are many things we can learn from the story of Mary,
but one thing is central. We are dealing here with the simple
fact of the Incarnation. God sent forth His Son to be born of a
woman. We see here the profound difference between a theophany and the Incarnation. In a theophany God appears tempo-
rarily in the form of a man even as the angel Gabriel may have
appeared to Mary. In the Incarnation, God becomes man. He
who meets us as the Son of Mary is at the same time fully God
and *fully man.*

*"We have found him of whom Moses in the law and
also the prophets wrote, Jesus of Nazareth, the son of
Joseph."—John 1:45, R.S.V.*

4. JOSEPH

Scripture background: Matthew 1 and 2; Luke 2.

Luke tells us that at one time when Jesus was preaching "a woman in the crowd raised her voice and said to him,
'Blessed is the womb that bore you, and the breasts that you
sucked!'" Jesus replied, "Blessed rather are those who hear the
word of God and keep it!" (Luke 11:27-28, R.S.V.) We can

understand the feelings of the woman who in her enthusiasm for Jesus pronounced a blessing on the woman who gave Him birth. But Jesus insists that more meaningful than the physical tie between Him and His mother is the spiritual bond between Him and all those who hear and keep the word of God.

We do not know when Joseph and Mary shared with the child Jesus the story of His miraculous birth. But the attitude expressed by Jesus in the incident to which we have just referred would lead us to think that the absence of the physical tie would not have made any difference to Him in His love for the man He called father. Jesus' contemporaries considered Him the son of Joseph. Philip says to Nathanael: "We have found him of whom Moses in the law and also the prophets wrote, Jesus of Nazareth, the son of Joseph." (John 1:45, R.S.V.) Nathanael makes no comment on Joseph, but he finds it difficult to believe that the Messiah has come out of Nazareth. Later when Jesus says to the Jews, "I am the bread which came down from heaven," they reply, "Is not this Jesus, the son of Joseph, whose father and mother we know?" (John 6:41-42.) When Jesus returns to Nazareth, the people say of Him, "Is not this the carpenter's son? Is not his mother called Mary? And are not his brothers James and Joseph and Simon and Judas? And are not all his sisters with us?" (Matthew 13:55-56, R.S.V.) When Joseph and Mary find Jesus in the Temple after a three-days' search, His mother says to Him: "Behold, your father and I have been looking for you anxiously." (Luke 2:48, R.S.V.) And when Luke describes the presentation in the Temple he says, "His father and his mother marveled at what was said about him." (Luke 2:33, R.S.V.) Luke gives the genealogy of Jesus according to Joseph but in this case qualifies his reference to Jesus as the son of Joseph with the phrase "as was supposed."

Both Matthew and Luke are perfectly clear in their teaching of the Virgin Birth. They are equally clear in their affirmation that Jesus was known as the son of Joseph. Jesus' knowledge of His origin must have been meaningful to Him as part of His characteristic consciousness of the uniqueness of His filial relation to

God. This doctrine of the Virgin Birth could not become meaningful to the Church, however, until mankind had first been confronted with the supreme mystery of the supernatural Person, with the wonder of God manifest in the flesh.

When Luke introduces us to Mary he says that she was "a virgin betrothed to a man whose name was Joseph, of the house of David." (Luke 1:27, R.S.V.) Matthew tells us of the revelation which came to Joseph. The dream through which God spoke to Joseph must have taken place shortly after Mary returned from her visit to Elisabeth. We are tempted to let our imagination play upon this scene and to seek to enter into the emotions and inner conflicts which must have gone on in the hearts of Joseph and Mary. But it is best to accept reverently the account given in Matthew 1:18-24 and not speculate too much on matters that are too wonderful for us. Joseph is described here as a righteous man whose justice is tempered with mercy and love. When Joseph receives the word of the Lord he responds in the obedience of faith. As Mary faces the word of Gabriel she says, "Behold I am the handmaid of the Lord; let it be to me according to your word." (Luke 1:38, R.S.V.) We do not have the response of Joseph, but we know that he accepted his place in the divine drama and remained obedient to the word that was spoken to him. In so doing he proved himself to be among those whom Jesus of Nazareth later claimed as His spiritual kin.

Joseph takes a leading part in the familiar stories connected with the birth of Jesus. He makes with Mary the trip from Nazareth to Bethlehem to register for the taxation ordered by Caesar Augustus. He is present when the baby Jesus is born in the stable in Bethlehem. He accompanies Mary some forty days later when Jesus is presented in the Temple. After the visit of the Wise Men he receives the angel's warning to flee with Mary and Jesus to Egypt. The stay in Egypt probably did not last more than a few months. Herod the Great died in April of that year, and Joseph returns before he hears that a son of Herod is reigning in Judea. In obedience to a word of the Lord received again in a dream Joseph took the mother and child and returned to the land

of Israel. Warned against settling in Judea, he made his way back
to Nazareth. The Herods were not likely to look for the Christ
child in Nazareth of Galilee.

In the home at Nazareth Joseph and Mary lived as man and
wife. Joseph became the carpenter of the village. With his daily
toil he made his living for his family. In time there were born into
the home four sons and at least two daughters. With Jesus, this
made a family of not less than seven children. It is well for us
to know that Jesus in the days of His flesh lived during most of
His life as part of a large family group. He had the experiences
of an older boy raised in a home filled with children.

We would like to know more of the relation of the boy Jesus
to the man Joseph. We can be sure that Joseph shared with Mary
the inability to fully understand this child. We know, too, that
Jesus accepted the discipline of the home and remained obedient
to Joseph and Mary. As the child Jesus increased in wisdom He
must have learned from Joseph the skills that fitted Him for His
life in a world in which He was known as the son of Joseph.

Joseph's last appearance in the New Testament narrative is in
connection with Jesus' visit to the Temple at the age of twelve.
The death of Joseph probably came some time before Jesus began
His public ministry at the age of thirty. The details are not known
to us, but it may be that Joseph left with Jesus the responsibility
of providing for the home until the younger children could take
care of themselves. He who was once known as the carpenter's
son became the carpenter of Nazareth. (Matthew 13:55; Mark
6:3.)

The world is not interested in the carpenter of Nazareth. The
world is interested in the Christ, the Son of the living God. But
if Jesus is acknowledged as the Son of God, then the world is interested in the fact that He of whom Moses wrote in the law and
the prophets lived among us as the carpenter of Nazareth. Jesus
in the days of His flesh passed through the whole range of human
experience. He was tested in all points like as we are. Because
He has entered our human life He knows how to sympathize with
us. He can be touched with a feeling of our infirmities. Part of

the bond between Jesus and the toiling masses of mankind is the knowledge that Jesus knew how to work with ax and saw, with hammer and plane. He is brother to all those who bear the burden of the world's work.

It is a tribute to Joseph that Jesus interpreted God in terms of fatherhood. He may have been dealing in memories of the home in Nazareth when He spoke of children asking for bread and not receiving a stone, of their asking for fish and not being given a serpent. Joseph was not a perfect man. There was in him as in all of us a mingling of good and evil. But he knew how to give good gifts to those who called him father. Was it not reasonable to suppose that the heavenly Father was able and willing to give good gifts to those who asked Him? Joseph knew the need of those who looked to him for food, for shelter, for clothing. He ministered to that need as best he could. Can we not pass from this experience of an earthly father to the trust in the Father in heaven who knows our needs before we ask Him? As we look at the home in Nazareth, can we not enter into the deeper meaning of the Old Testament word:

"As a father pities his children,
    so the Lord pities those who fear him.
For he knows our frame;
    he remembers that we are dust."
(Psalm 103:13-14, R.S.V.)

It is in the eternal relation of the Father to the Son that we know that fatherhood is at the heart of the existence of God. Our human fatherhoods are at best but a dim reflection of the Fatherhood at the heart of our universe, but they are the basis upon which we can begin to understand the love of the Father in heaven.

When Jesus interpreted God in terms of fatherhood He laid on all earthly parents the responsibility of seeking to build homes like the home in Nazareth, homes in which the children can pass from the experiences of the home to the knowledge of the God who has loved us and has sent unto us His Son.

"Waiting for the consolation of Israel."—Luke 2:25.

5. SIMEON

Scripture background: Luke 2:22-35.

Simeon was an old man who knew that he did not have many years left to him, but he had something to live for which gave meaning and purpose to his life. He knew that he would not see death until after he had seen the Lord's Christ.

Simeon was a righteous man. As he was drawing near to the end of his life he could look back upon long years in which he had stood for righteousness. He was also a devout man. He had accepted the faith of Israel and his life had been lived out in the fear of the Lord. There have been moral men who made no profession of religious faith, and there have been pious men who were not good men. But usually the man of faith is also the man of character. As he writes of Simeon, Luke says, "and the Holy Spirit was upon him." (Luke 2:25, R.S.V.) This man carried with him the sense of the presence of God. Those who knew Simeon felt that the Spirit of God was upon him.

Simeon was "waiting for the consolation of Israel." He shared with his people the hope that God would some day send to Israel One who would be known as the Lord's Anointed. Simeon was not alone in watching and waiting for the coming of the Christ. The expectancy of a coming Messiah was one of the characteristics of the Jews of his time. This hope of Israel for the coming of the Christ was not without foundations. It was grounded in the promises of God which had been made unto their fathers. The Jews give expression to this hope when they question John the Baptist concerning the authority of his message. They say to him, "Who art thou? . . . Art thou Elias? . . . Art thou that prophet?" (John 1:19-21.) The woman of Samaria expresses the same hope when she says, "I know that Messias cometh, which is called Christ: when he is come, he will tell us all things." (John

4:25.) Messianic expectancy burned at white heat in the Judaism of the first century.

Simeon shared the hope of his people, but in him the expectancy of the coming of the Christ was held with peculiar intensity. He lived in the days when the corruption of the Maccabean kingdom was apparent to all. A son of Edom sat on the throne of Judah. Simeon's people were a conquered people. The Roman yoke was heavy, and from a human point of view there was no hope that Israel would be able to regain her freedom. He knew the moral corruption of the time. In the midst of the evil of his world he cried out for the coming of the Lord's Anointed. His prayer was that the Christ would come in his lifetime and that before death his eyes might rest on the Messiah of his people.

His prayer had been heard. The Holy Spirit had promised him that he would not see death until he had seen the Christ. He knew that he was nearing the end of his pilgrimage and that the coming of death was not far away. He knew also that before he saw death he would see the long-expected Messiah. This gave a note of urgency to his waiting for the coming of the Christ. While living in this expectancy, Simeon was inspired of the Spirit to enter the Temple. As he did so, his eyes fell on a peasant couple from Galilee who had with them a baby boy less than two months old.

This visit to the Temple had been undertaken by Joseph and Mary in obedience to the law of their people. The visit combined both the rite of ceremonial purification of the mother and the rite of redemption of the first-born. (Exodus 13:2, 12; Leviticus 12:2-8.) Jesus was circumcised on the eighth day in accordance with the law. He received in His flesh the sign and seal of the Abrahamic covenant. The rite of the redemption of the first-born pointed back to the Exodus, to the time when the angel of death destroyed the first-born of Egypt but passed over the first-born of Israel. In the care with which the details of the requirements of the law were observed in the birth of Jesus we can see the force of Paul's statement: "When the time had fully come, God sent forth his Son, born of woman, *born under the law*." (Galatians 4:4, R.S.V.) The law required as part of the rite of purification of the mother the offering of a lamb for a burnt offering and a pigeon or a dove for a sin offering. It permitted, however, those who could not afford a lamb to substitute a pigeon or a dove. Joseph and Mary brought the offering of the poor.

When the eyes of Simeon fall on the baby Jesus, it is revealed to him that this child is the Lord's Christ. The old man takes the baby in his arms. As he holds the child, the Holy Spirit comes upon him, and he blesses God as he utters prophetic words which interpret for all ages the significance of the birth of this child. We have first his expression of his readiness for death now that his eyes have seen the Christ according to the promise of the Lord. Then he says: "Mine eyes have seen thy salvation, which thou hast prepared before the face of all people." He knows that God through this child has acted decisively for the providing of a salvation which shall be available to all mankind.

Simeon goes on to say that the child he holds in his arms will be "a light to lighten the Gentiles." (The Revised Standard Version gives it more accurately, "a light for revelation to the Gentiles.") It may seem surprising that Simeon, who was intensely a Jew, "waiting for the consolation of Israel," should have seen in Jesus, God's salvation which He had prepared *in the presence of all peoples* and should have predicted that Jesus would be "a light for revelation to the Gentiles." But we take a narrow view of Israel's hope when we limit that hope to the yearning for the redemption of Israel. At the very heart of Israel's faith there was the expectancy that God through the Hebrew people would prepare a salvation for all mankind. The Abrahamic covenant was established with the promise that through the seed of Abraham all the nations of the earth would be blessed. (Genesis 22:18.) The great prophets had consistently said that the purpose of God reached through Israel to the whole earth. (Isaiah 45:22.) Paul never tired of pointing out to his contemporaries the universal nature of Israel's hope. Through the birth of Jesus the nations of the earth have received the revelation which has given them their knowledge of God's character and of the duty which God requires of man.

Simeon sees also that Jesus is the glory of Israel. He may have meant by this that Jesus was the noblest of the sons of Israel. This is high praise. Israel has given us such men as Moses, David, Isaiah, Peter, John, and Paul; but who would doubt that Jesus of Nazareth is Israel's noblest gift to the world? He is indeed the glory of Israel. Simeon may have meant that the true glory of Israel was to be found in the way she accomplished her task of preparing the way for the coming of the Christ. The Christ could not have come apart from Israel, and apart from Israel He could not have been understood.

Simeon returns the child to His mother and proceeds to address Mary in prophetic words which tell us much of the destiny of her Son. He says that this child is to be God's sign to man. Jesus is to be the One who points us to God and to the resurrection world of God which lies beyond our human existence. But he says also that Jesus is to be a sign "which shall be spoken against." To Simeon there was given the knowledge that the child who came as a revelation of God to man would so arouse the fears and prejudices of men that the people of His generation would unite to destroy Him. As Simeon looks at Mary he says: "A sword shall pierce through thy own soul also." The mother is to suffer as she sees the things which are done to her Son. In prophetic vision, the old man sees the time when the sorrowing mother shall stand in the presence of her crucified Son.

Simeon sees also that this child is set for the fall and the rising of many in Israel. He knows that the Israel which is according to the flesh will find in Jesus of Nazareth a stone of stumbling and a rock of offense. He predicts Israel's rejection of her Messiah. But he knows also that through this child there will be brought into being the new Israel, the Israel of God, the redeemed community which will become the instrument of God's redemptive purpose for all mankind.

Simeon says that through the suffering of the Christ the thoughts of many hearts will be revealed. He knew that in their response to the suffering Messiah men would reveal their inmost thoughts. Those who loved the truth would come to Him, and those who were committed to evil would shrink back from Him. By their reaction to Jesus men would reveal themselves.

> *"There was a prophetess, Anna . . . and . . . she . . . spoke of him to all who were looking for the redemption of Jerusalem."*—Luke 2:36-38, R.S.V.

6. ANNA

Scripture background: Luke 2:22-38.

The center of interest in the story of the presentation of Jesus at the Temple is the prophecy of Simeon. But Luke follows this story with two verses in which he calls our attention to a woman named Anna. The first thing he tells us about her is that she was a prophetess. Plummer comments: "She was known as such [i.e., as a prophetess] before this occasion. Like Miriam, Deborah, Huldah, and the daughters of Philip, Anna was a woman divinely inspired to make known God's will to others."* We notice also that she was of the tribe of Asher. The northern tribes had been carried into captivity, but there were probably many of the Jews of the first century who traced their ancestry back to one of the lost tribes. Anna was a woman of great age. She had been married and had lived for seven years with her husband. After his death, she had lived the rest of her life as a widow. The Greek text does not indicate clearly whether the 84 years is to be taken as her age at this time or as the number of years she had lived as a widow. In either case she could be described as aged. Anna was a devout woman who attended regularly the services of worship in the Temple. She may actually have lived in the Temple, but more probably she lived near the Temple and spent most of her time there.

* Alfred Plummer, *The International Critical Commentary on Luke*, p. 72. New York: Charles Scribner's Sons. By permission.

Anna may have heard the prophecy of Simeon concerning the baby Jesus, or she may have come into the Temple just as Simeon finished speaking. When she saw the infant Jesus, the spirit of prophecy came upon her. The Holy Spirit revealed unto her the unique significance of this child. Anna's first reaction was to offer up a prayer of thanksgiving to God. Luke tells us also that she "spoke of him [i.e., of the baby] to all who were looking for the redemption of Jerusalem." (Luke 2:38, R.S.V.)

Why did Luke feel that this incident was of sufficient importance for him to preserve it as the sequel to his account of the prophecy of Simeon? We cannot be perfectly sure of our answer, but it is probable that Luke preserves this story because in it the baby Jesus is identified with the hope for the redemption of Jerusalem.

David made Jerusalem the capital of his empire. He brought the ark of the Lord, the visible symbol of Jehovah's presence with His people, to Jerusalem. Solomon carried out the purposes of his father in building the Temple at Jerusalem and placing the ark in the Holy of Holies. From this time on, Jerusalem became identified with the religious life of the people. When the kingdom was divided, devout Jews felt that the religion of the northern tribes was corrupt because it was not centered in the Temple at Jerusalem.

When the children of Judah were carried into captivity in Babylon, the exiles yearned for the restoration of Jerusalem. The writer of Psalm 137 cries out:

> "If I forget you, O Jerusalem,
>   let my right hand wither!
> Let my tongue cleave to the roof of my mouth,
>   if I do not remember you,
> if I do not set Jerusalem
>   above my highest joy!"
>   (Psalm 137:5-6, R.S.V.)

And the Jews never forgot the rejoicing of the Edomites at the

fall of Jerusalem. This is reflected in verse 7 of the same Psalm.
The writer says:

"Remember, O Lord, against the Edomites
the day of Jerusalem,
how they said, 'Rase it, rase it!
Down to its foundations!' "

When Anna prayed for the redemption of Jerusalem she was
probably concerned for the political deliverance of the sacred
city. She would have approved of the prayer of Zacharias that
the Lord of Israel would grant

"that we, being delivered from the hand of our enemies,
might serve him without fear,
in holiness and righteousness before him all the days of
our life."

(Luke 1:74-75, R.S.V.)

Anna could not forget that a son of Edom sat on the throne of
Judah and ruled as a tyrant.

But we can be sure that Anna's deepest concern was not for
the political deliverance of Jerusalem. She had spent most of her
life in the Temple as a prophetess of the Lord. She could not have
been ignorant of the corruption of the religious life of Israel. She
must have seen the hypocrisy and self-righteousness of the scribes
and Pharisees, and have known the way in which the office of
high priest had been degraded until it was determined almost
entirely by the test of political expediency. This righteous woman
yearned for the coming of One who would purify the sons of
Levi. She looked for a Jerusalem that could be the true religious
center of the life of her people. Anna was not alone in her hope
for the cleansing of Israel's religious life. The reference to "all
who were looking for the redemption of Jerusalem" would suggest that she was associated with a number of people who shared
her concern.

To what extent did Jesus fulfill the hope of Anna and those
associated with her? Jesus shared with Anna the love of Jerusalem
as the center of the life of His people. When He came to Jerusa-

lem as a boy of twelve, He recognized the Temple as His Father's house. When His parents lost Him, after three days they found Him in the Temple with the teachers of the law. Jesus' love for Jerusalem underlies and gives meaning to the well-known lament over the city. (Matthew 23:37-39.) We are told of two times when Jesus burst into tears. One of these was in connection with the death of Lazarus (John 11:35), and the other, during the Triumphal Entry, was an expression of His sorrow as He looked upon Jerusalem (Luke 19:41).

The love which Jesus had for Jerusalem did not prevent Him from realizing the chasm between the existing Jerusalem and the Jerusalem which might have been the true center of the faith of Israel. There is rare irony in His words to Herod: "It cannot be that a prophet perish out of Jerusalem." (Luke 13:33.) It is in this connection that Luke records the words: "O Jerusalem, Jerusalem, killing the prophets and stoning those who are sent to you! How often would I have gathered your children together as a hen gathers her brood under her wings, and you would not!" (Luke 13:34, R.S.V.)

In His conversation with the woman of Samaria, Jesus irrevocably cuts the tie between Jerusalem and her Temple, and the purity of the worship of the Lord. The woman says: "Our fathers worshiped on this mountain; and you say that in Jerusalem is the place where men ought to worship." (John 4:20, R.S.V.) Jesus replies: "Woman, believe me, the hour is coming when neither on this mountain nor in Jerusalem will you worship the Father. . . . God is spirit, and those who worship him must worship in spirit and truth." (John 4:21-24, R.S.V.)

Jesus clearly predicted the destruction of both the city and the Temple. He pointed to the stones of the Temple and said: "The days will come when there shall not be left here one stone upon another that will not be thrown down." (Luke 21:5, R.S.V.) He said also that Jerusalem would be trodden down by the Gentiles. (Luke 21:24.)

There seems to be little to justify the hope of Anna that this child would be the One to bring about the political deliverance of Jerusalem. But if we understand the hope of Anna on its deepest level we can see that it was not disappointed. Anna was concerned for the redemption of Jerusalem as the religious center of her people. Although Jesus was rejected by His own people, He did call into being a new Israel, a new believing community which was destined to be the medium of the proclamation of the message of salvation to the ends of the earth. The Jerusalem which Anna knew disappeared, but the Christian community seized upon the concept of Jerusalem to present their hope of "a house not made with hands, eternal in the heavens." (2 Corinthians 5:1, R.S.V.) The New Testament closes with the picture of the new Jerusalem coming down out of heaven as a bride adorned for her husband. Of this Jerusalem it could be said: "There shall in no wise enter into it any thing that defileth, neither whatsoever worketh abomination, or maketh a lie: but they which are written in the Lamb's book of life." (Revelation 21:27.)

The heart of Anna's hope was for the redemption of the religious community. The need for this hope is still with us. There is always a chasm between the Church which actually exists and the Church which could have been brought into being if Christians had surrendered more completely to Jesus as Saviour and Lord. Jesus Christ confronts His Church today as He confronted the Jerusalem of His own time. If His Church responds to His call she becomes the instrument of His redemptive purpose. But the Church which has ceased to hear her Master's voice will be left as desolate as the Jerusalem of the first century.

"Jesus was born in Bethlehem of Judaea in the days of Herod the king . . ."—Matthew 2:1.

7.   HEROD THE GREAT

Scripture background: Matthew 2.

The statement that Jesus was born in Bethlehem in the days of Herod the king gives the information necessary to date with some accuracy the time of His birth. We know from secular history that Herod died in the year of Rome 750, about the time of the Passover. The Passover came in April, and if we place the birth of Jesus some months before this to allow time for the presentation in the Temple and the flight into Egypt, we will reach a date not far from the commonly accepted December 25. The actual day of the year is, of course, unknown. By a mistake in calculation at the time that the Christian calendar was established, the date of the birth of Jesus was misplaced by four years. But we cannot now correct all the dates of history. We must therefore content ourselves with the seemingly contradictory statement that Jesus was born in the year 4 B.C. This explains also the statement that He was thirty-three years old and died at the time of the Passover in the year A.D. 30.

More important than the effort to be completely accurate about the date is the understanding that we are dealing here with an event which takes place at a definite location—Bethlehem of Judea—and at a definite time—in the days of Herod the king.

The Herod who is mentioned here is Herod the Great. He is the only actor closely connected with the birth of the Christ, who is also known to us in secular history. Luke places Jesus' birth at the time of the first enrollment, which was by decree of Caesar Augustus and was taken when Cyrenius was governor of Syria. The birth of Jesus is therefore given its setting in world history. Neither Caesar Augustus nor Cyrenius appears in the Nativity stories, but Herod attempts to destroy the infant Messiah. The story of Herod reveals God's providential care of the Christ. Herod seeks to find and destroy the infant Christ. The power of the throne is directed against a baby born in a manger; but God speaks in a dream to the Wise Men, and the angel of the Lord speaks the word of warning to Joseph. Herod is mocked of the Wise Men, and in his wrath he sends his soldiers on a mission of ruthless slaughter. But the soldiers of Herod do not find the infant Jesus. We are reminded of the words of the Second Psalm: "The kings of the earth set themselves, and the rulers take counsel together, against the Lord, and against his anointed"; and the comment of the psalmist: "He that sitteth in the heavens shall laugh: the Lord shall have them in derision." (Psalm 2:2, 4.)

The career of Herod is well known to students of history. He was the son of Antipater, a ruler of Edom who was a friend and ally of Rome. Both his father and his mother were descendants of Esau. About 125 B.C. John Hyrcanus had conquered Edom and had forced its people to receive circumcision and to accept nominally the Jewish faith. The Romans considered the Herods as native princes of the Jews, but the Jews never forgot that these rulers were sons of Edom. Herod became king of Judea after his capture of Jerusalem with the aid of the Romans in 37 B.C. He proved himself to be a ruthless but able ruler. Supported by the Romans, he brought most of Palestine into one kingdom. In order to appease the Jews, he rebuilt the Temple at Jerusalem. The Temple of Jesus' day was known as Herod's Temple.

Herod was unfortunate in his domestic life. To him, marriage was a road to power. Before he became king of Judea he married a woman named Doris who bore him his first-born son, named Antipater for Herod's father. Shortly before the capture of Jerusalem he married the beautiful and chaste Mariamne, granddaughter of Hyrcanus. This marriage was an act of expediency in which Herod sought to ally himself by marriage with the Maccabean kings. The sons Mariamne bore him, Alexander and Aristobulus, would in this way have stood as descendants of the Hasmonean dynasty. But the life of Herod was not to be marked by domestic peace. He followed the pattern of other Oriental monarchs and married ten wives in all. Mariamne hated him because of his cruelty to other members of her family, and Herod had her put to death in 29 B.C. About three years before the birth of Jesus he also executed her sons Alexander and Aristobulus. His suspicion then fell on Antipater, who had poisoned his mind against the sons of Mariamne. When the Wise Men came to Jerusalem, Antipater also was in prison. Later he was executed by Herod's command just a few days before Herod's own death. When the king knew that his time of death was near he knew also that he was hated by his people. He left the order that a number of the leading citizens of Judea should be executed at the time of his death in order that this might be a time of mourning. This infamous order was never carried out.

When we see the hates and fears of Herod we can easily understand that he was aroused by the report that there had been born in Bethlehem of Judea a son of David who was destined to be the king of the Jews. Here also Herod acts with his usual craftiness. He tells the Wise Men to seek diligently for the young child until they find Him. Herod says: "Bring me word again, that I may come and worship him also." (Matthew 2:8.) But in his heart is the intention to destroy this child before He can become the center of the messianic aspirations of His people.

When we study the picture of Herod which is given here, we realize again the statement that men who rule by terror live in terror. Herod could trust neither the wife of his bosom nor the sons who came forth from his loins. He trusted no one and no one trusted him. He lived in constant fear of dying as his father had done, at the hands of an assassin. In this, Herod was not different from other tyrants. Adolf Hitler at the zenith of his power lived in terror of those who would take his life. Judge John J. Parker, who was present at the Nuremberg trials, said that there was not one of those men who would not have turned white if he had heard an unexpected knock at the door at 2 A.M. He who rules by terror lives in terror. And every man who begins to use for his sinful purposes those who are evil, finds that in the end he is surrounded by people he cannot trust.

Herod set out to establish a dynasty, but he did not have the moral integrity necessary to establish a throne that would be the instrument of justice. He and his descendants ruled in Judea for a period of about a hundred years. Some of the Herods were bold and brave, but all of them were crafty and bad. The permanence of the throne is established by righteousness, but Herod knew nothing of this kind of concern for justice.

We see therefore in sharp contrast the kingdom of the Herods and the Kingdom which Jesus came to establish. The Herods ruled by terror. Jesus built His Kingdom on love. He also proclaimed Himself as Lord and Master. The loyalty which He sought was the loving response of men to His love for them. There is a sense in which His Kingdom is not in this world. As our risen Lord, He sits upon the throne of the universe. But He calls forth the loyalties of men who freely acknowledge Him as Lord. In this sense the Kingdom which Jesus came to establish transcends all the loyalties of earth. In the words of the angel Gabriel to Mary: "Jesus . . . shall reign over the house of Jacob for ever; and of his kingdom there shall be no end." (Luke 1:31, 33.)

Faces Along the Way

"Behold, I send my messenger before thy face . . ."—
Mark 1:2.
"A man sent from God, whose name was John."—
John 1:6.

8. JOHN THE BAPTIST

Scripture background: Matthew 3:1-12; 11:1-9; 21:23-27, 32; Mark 1:1-15; 6:14-29; 11:27-33; Luke 1:1-25, 57:80; 3:1-22; 7:17-34; John 1:6-9, 15-36; 3:23-36; 10:40-41; Acts 13:24-25; 18:25; 19:1-7.

He who would tell the story of Jesus must start with the ministry of John. As Luke places the beginning of the preaching of John in the fifteenth year of Tiberius Caesar, we have a firm basis in history for our study of the story of Jesus. John and Jesus were associated in their birth. John was born about six months before Jesus. There is no reason to think that John and Jesus were together in their youth. Jesus grew up in the home of the carpenter of Nazareth. John was in the desert until the day of his showing. Jesus and John were different in their personalities. John was an ascetic. He was a Nazarite from his birth. In contrast, Jesus came eating and drinking. John lived alone in the desert. Jesus lived in a normal family situation and worked as a carpenter. John was the prophet of righteousness and judgment. Jesus could speak in stern notes of condemnation, but He was also a man of compassion and tenderness. Jesus was deeply interested in John. He pronounced him the greatest of the prophets and as more than a prophet—as the messenger sent by God to prepare the way for the Christ.

John came into the country about Jordan preaching the baptism of repentance for the remission of sins. He came under a deep sense of mission. In him the voice of prophecy which had been silent for centuries reappeared. He was the last of the prophets to proclaim that the time for the coming of the Christ was at hand.

John's message was a call to repentance. Nothing is easier than a call to repentance which does not deal in specific sins. Nothing is more searching than a genuine experience of repentance in which we see the evil of our ways and turn from our sins unto God. John dealt in specifics. He told the people that they could no longer trust in their descent from Abraham as the basis of their acceptance with God. He told the publicans that they could exact no more than that which was appointed to them. He told the soldiers that they could not deal in violence or in false accusation. And he had the courage to tell Herod the king that it was not lawful for him to have taken for his wife Herodias, the wife of his brother Philip. For this he earned the undying hatred of Herodias. His boldness in rebuking the morals of the king led in the end to his imprisonment and death.

John's call to repentance involved more than the rebuke of sin as the violation of the moral law. John called upon men to repent because the Christ was at hand. He knew that the coming of the Christ would be for individuals and for the nation a time of decision and judgment. The sins John condemned were acts of disobedience to God which were certain in time to bring judgment. They were seen in their darkest hues when they rendered men unable or unwilling to recognize the Christ. The sin which prevents a man from finding his place in the Kingdom of God may mean that he misses his opportunity for eternal life. In the main, the people who received the baptism of John were the people who recognized Jesus, and the groups which rejected the message of John were to be found in opposition to Jesus. Herod Antipas himself was at one time deeply affected by the preaching of John. (Mark 6:20.) But after he had hardened his heart in the execution of John, he stood in the presence of a greater than John and was moved only by idle curiosity. The nation which failed to heed

John's call to repentance was the nation which rejected its Messiah.

John fanned into a white heat the Messianic expectancy of his time. He made it clear that he was not the Christ. He said that he was not worthy to unloose the latchet of the shoes of the One who was coming after him. He knew that he could only baptize with water and that the One who was coming would baptize with the Holy Spirit and with fire. When Jesus came, John pointed his own disciples to Him as the Son of God, as the Lamb of God who takes away the sin of the world. (John 1:29.) Jesus chose the core of His band of disciples from the followers of John.

Jesus was baptized by John. It was in this experience that John came to know with certainty who Jesus was. John had hesitated to administer baptism to Jesus, but Jesus insisted. In receiving baptism from John, He expressed His public approval of John's ministry. He did not receive baptism as an admission of sin or as an expression of His need for salvation. He probably did express through His baptism His identification of Himself with mankind. The baptism of Jesus marks the dividing line between His private life and His public ministry. Later Jesus made baptism the outward and visible sign of identification with the Christian Church.

After the baptism of Jesus, John continued for a time his ministry of preaching. When he was baptizing in Aenon near Salim, some of his disciples came to him and said: "Rabbi, he that was with thee beyond Jordan, to whom thou barest witness, behold, the same baptizeth, and all men come to him. John answered and said, A man can receive nothing, except it be given him from heaven. Ye yourselves bear me witness, that I said, I am not the Christ, but that I am sent before him. He that hath the bride is the bridegroom: but the friend of the bridegroom, which standeth and heareth him, rejoiceth greatly because of the bridegroom's voice: this my joy therefore is fulfilled. He must increase, but I must decrease." (John 3:26-30.) John's greatness lay in his willingness to decrease that Jesus might increase.

It cannot have been long after this that John was arrested and cast into prison. In prison he experienced a moment of uncertainty. It may have rooted in his own difficulty in adjusting to the life of a prisoner, or perhaps in the fact that Jesus did not seem to be the kind of Messiah that John was expecting. Even John must have found it difficult to accept the idea of a suffering Messiah. He sent two of his disciples to Jesus, saying, "Art thou he that should come, or do we look for another?" (Matthew 11:3.) Jesus did not give a direct answer to this question. Instead He sent the disciples back to report the things they had seen and heard and to say to John: "Blessed is he, whosoever shall not be offended in me." (Matthew 11:6.) This is an indirect answer indicating that John in his moment of uncertainty must face the evidence and make his response of faith. We can be sure that John did not permanently find an occasion of stumbling in Jesus.

As Jesus was teaching in the Temple a few days before His death, the chief priests and elders came to Him and said: "By what authority doest thou these things? and who gave thee this authority?" And Jesus answered, "I also will ask you one thing, which if ye tell me, I in like wise will tell you by what authority I do these things. The baptism of John, whence was it? from heaven, or of men? And they reasoned with themselves, saying, If we shall say, From heaven; he will say unto us, Why did ye not then believe him? But if we shall say, Of men; we fear the people; for all hold John as a prophet. And they answered Jesus, and said, We cannot tell. And he said unto them, Neither tell I you by what authority I do these things." (Matthew 21:23-27.) It is easy to see that Jesus asked a catch question. The chief priests and elders were in trouble regardless of how they answered it. The dilemma of the leaders of the Jews is also a tribute to John's tremendous influence over the common people. The chief priests were afraid of being stoned at the hands of the mob if they suggested that John was not a true prophet. When we see the intensity of this feeling we can have some understanding of the fact that twenty years later in another section of the world there were still those who were proclaiming the baptism of John. (Acts 18:25; 19:1-7.)

Jesus did not raise an irrelevant question when He asked about the baptism of John. John had come without any external authentication. He had not performed any miracles. (John 10:41.) He had come like the prophet of old as the bearer of the word of God. And the proof that his contemporaries had of the truth of his message was that the things he had said of Jesus came to pass. John had spoken to the consciences of men, and he had depended on the Spirit of God to drive home the truth of his message. The leaders of the Jews had been unable to receive him because there had been in them a lack of moral earnestness. The inability of these people to receive the baptism of John was a sign that they were also unable to understand the authority of Jesus.

Jesus did perform miracles; but He was not interested in the faith of those who believed on Him only because they had seen His miracles. (John 2:23-24.) In the last analysis His authority lay in His power to authenticate Himself to those who were genuinely seeking the truth. He could make Himself known to those who were willing to surrender to Him in love and obedience, but He remained a stumbling block to those who loved darkness rather than light because their deeds were evil.

It is in this sense that Jesus confronts the men and women who meet Him in the pages of the New Testament. He gives to those who receive Him the power to become the children of God. He remains an occasion of offense to those who will not come to Him that they may have life. The risen Lord still confronts us as the Eternal Contemporary of every man and every age. He speaks to us through the pages of the New Testament and makes Himself known to those who will receive Him. To others, He remains a stumbling block.

*"Except a man be born again, he cannot see the king-
dom of God."—John 3:3.*

9.   NICODEMUS

*Scripture   background: John   2:23;   3:1-21;   7:40-53;
19:38-42.*

In verses 23-25 of his second chapter, John tells us of a
visit of Jesus to Jerusalem at the time of the Passover. He says
that there were many who believed on Jesus when they saw the
miracles which He did. Jesus did not commit Himself to them,
for He knew that they had a speculative faith based on their reaction to His mighty works. He knew also that their faith did not
involve surrender to Him as Lord and Master. As an example of
the faith which Jesus could not accept, John tells us the story of
Nicodemus.

Nicodemus was a Pharisee. He belonged to the group within
Judaism which was outstanding in its patriotism and religious
zeal. He was a ruler of the Jews. When we combine this reference
with the place which Nicodemus evidently held in the councils
of the Jews as revealed in John 7:50, we are probably safe in saying that Nicodemus was a member of the Sanhedrin. In verse 10
of the third chapter Jesus refers to Nicodemus as "the teacher of
Israel." (A.S.V.) Evidently Nicodemus was recognized as a scholar
and a leader of his people.

Why did this man come to Jesus? He came because he and
many of those associated with him were convinced that Jesus was
a teacher sent from God. Evidently Nicodemus had either witnessed some of the miracles of Jesus or had received reliable information about them from those who had seen them. He had
become convinced that Jesus must be a teacher sent from God
because he knew that no man could do the mighty works which
Jesus did unless God was with Him. In his sermon at Pentecost,

Peter could refer to Jesus as "a man approved of God among you by miracles and wonders and signs, which God did by him in the midst of you, as ye yourselves also know." (Acts 2:22.) Nicodemus came to Jesus because he was convinced that Jesus was a teacher sent from God.

Nicodemus came to Him by night. It is interesting to notice that in the three places in which Nicodemus is mentioned in Scripture he is characterized as the man who came to Jesus by night. Evidently he came by night because he did not want to be seen. He wanted to talk with Jesus but he did not want his friends to know about the visit.

Jesus knows that Nicodemus has come by night because he is unwilling to come in the day. He confronts Nicodemus with the blunt statement: "Except a man be born again, he cannot see the kingdom of God." In his prologue John has said of Jesus: "He came unto his own, and his own received him not. But as many as received him, to them gave he power to become the sons of God, even to them that believe on his name: which were born, not of blood, nor of the will of the flesh, nor of the will of man, but of God." (John 1:11-13.) The capacity to become sons of God is given by God to those who receive Jesus Christ. To clarify His statement Jesus says to Nicodemus: "Except a man be born of water and of the Spirit, he cannot enter into the kingdom of God." Born of the Spirit refers to the work of God's Holy Spirit as He creates a new life in those who receive Jesus. Born of water probably refers to baptism as the act of public identification with the followers of Jesus. If this interpretation of Jesus' meaning is correct, we can say that He makes two demands on Nicodemus. The first is the inner act of surrender to Him as Lord. It is this receiving of Jesus which is related to the redemptive act of the Spirit in the heart. Jesus asks also for open confession.

Nicodemus has no intention of meeting either of these demands. He has come by night that he might enter into conversation with Jesus. He has a speculative faith in Jesus as a teacher sent from God. But he has no intention of identifying himself with Jesus in surrender to Him as Lord. Nicodemus hopes to carry on a discussion with Jesus in which he is a detached spectator. He wishes to sit in the balcony and discuss the issues of life, but he has no desire to leave the balcony for the road and become deeply involved in life's pilgrimage. Jesus tells Nicodemus that from the detached point of view of the spectator it is impossible for him to understand the simplest truths of the Kingdom of God. Jesus has talked to Nicodemus of the necessity of regeneration, of the inward act of faith and the outward act of confession. Nicodemus has not understood these "earthly things"; how, then, can he understand the deepest mysteries of the Kingdom of God? How can he understand heavenly things?

As their conversation continues, Jesus opens to Nicodemus some of the central truths of the Christian faith. He draws aside the veil which hides the heart of God and discloses the counsels of the eternal God. He reveals the truths which man cannot discover for himself. He tells Nicodemus things which man can never know unless he is told them by One who has come down from heaven.

As He talks to Nicodemus, Jesus speaks the famous sixteenth verse of the third chapter of John. He says: "God so loved the world, that he gave his only begotten Son, that whosoever believeth in him should not perish, but have everlasting life." Jesus tells Nicodemus that God Himself could not redeem mankind without giving Himself in suffering love. This is the vast difference between the God of the Bible and the God of Greek philosophy. The Greeks thought of God as a detached observer of human life. The God who comes to us in Jesus Christ *loves us* so much that He *gives* His only begotten Son to die for us.

Jesus reminds Nicodemus of an Old Testament story which must have been well known to him. It is found in Numbers 21:4-9. During their journey through the wilderness the people were bitten by fiery serpents. Moses, in obedience to the command of the Lord, lifted up a brazen serpent with the promise that those who looked to the serpent when they were bitten would live. Jesus tells Nicodemus that as Moses lifted up the serpent in the wilderness, even so must the Son of man be lifted up that whosoever believeth in Him should not perish, but have everlasting life. The reference is, of course, to His death on the cross and to the divine appointment through which His death is an act of expiation for the sin of the world. Jesus makes it very clear to Nicodemus that those who believe in the Son are to receive eternal life and that those who refuse to receive the Son remain revealed and condemned.

Nicodemus must have gone away from this meeting with Jesus in a state of confusion and uncertainty. He had come for a speculative conversation in which he himself was not to be too deeply involved, but Jesus confronted him with His claims for decision and obedience. Nicodemus was not able to understand the earthly things of which Jesus spoke so clearly; and certainly he was not able, from the point of view of the spectator, to understand the profound truths of revelation which Jesus disclosed.

Some months later Jesus was again in Jerusalem. By this time the opposition to Him had hardened. The Pharisees and the chief priests send officers to arrest Jesus. (John 7:32.) A little later they return without Him. When the soldiers are asked why they have failed to make the arrest they say: "Never man spake like this man." Nicodemus is a member of the tribunal which had been expecting to sit in judgment on Jesus. He knows that Jesus is a teacher sent from God, but he is numbered with the enemies of Jesus. He is finding that it is not easy to maintain the position of a neutral. There may be a sly thrust at Nicodemus when the members of the Sanhedrin say to the officers: "Have any of the rulers or of the Pharisees believed on him?" Some of them may have heard of the secret visit of their colleague. Nicodemus attempts a weak defense. He says: "Doth our law judge any man, before it hear him, and know what he doeth?" (John 7:51.) The appeal is to a point of law and procedure. It is not a defense of Jesus, but the leaders of the Jews are in no mood to take patiently even this kind of questioning. They silence Nicodemus with the words: "Art thou also of Galilee? Search, and look: for out of Galilee ariseth no prophet." With this parting thrust at Nicodemus they go home.

Nicodemus was probably not present when the Sanhedrin under the leadership of Caiaphas pronounced Jesus as guilty of blasphemy and worthy of death. If he was present he must have kept quiet. We can be sure that he felt keenly the deed of shame in which the hierarchy in Jerusalem put to death Jesus of Nazareth. Nicodemus had a friend named Joseph of Arimathaea. The two men had much in common. They both believed in Jesus, and neither of them was willing to confess his faith openly. Joseph was afraid he would lose his wealth. Nicodemus was afraid he would lose his prestige. But after it was known that Jesus was dead, Joseph went boldly to Pilate and begged the body of Jesus. Nicodemus was not with him; but when he heard that the request of Joseph had been granted, he at last ceased to take counsel of his fears. He came bringing a mixture of myrrh and aloes for the anointing of the body.

Nicodemus stood with Joseph at the foot of the cross and looked upon the lifeless body of Jesus. As he saw the crucified Christ, the conversation on the night he came to Jesus must have come back to him. Jesus had spoken of a God who loved us enough to give His Son to die for us. Nicodemus had not understood what He was talking about. Jesus had said that the Son of man must be lifted up from the earth as Moses lifted up the serpent in the wilderness, that whosoever would believe in Him might not perish. His words had not made sense to Nicodemus, but as he looked at the dead Christ on the cross he began to understand. We do not know what happened to Nicodemus. Our last vision of him is as he and Joseph bear the body of Jesus to the tomb. But we can be reasonably certain that the coming to the cross was at last his leap of faith in which he left the position of the spectator and became a committed follower of One whom he had known all along was a teacher sent from God.

"If thou knewest the gift of God, and who it is that saith to thee, Give me to drink; thou wouldest have asked of him, and he would have given thee living water."—John 4:10.

10.   A WOMAN OF SAMARIA

Scripture background: John 4:1-42.

The woman of Samaria was surprised when Jesus asked her for a drink. She knew the deep-seated prejudices which separated the Jews and the Samaritans, and she was amazed that a man who was a Jew should ask a favor of a woman of Samaria. As a woman of Samaria she understood the long argument between the Jews and the Samaritans over the proper place of worship. The depth of feeling on the part of the Samaritans is shown by the way in which the Samaritans on another occasion refuse to receive Jesus because His face is "as though he would go to Jerusalem." (Luke 9:53.) As a Samaritan, this woman shares with the Jews the hope of the coming of the Messiah. She can say to Jesus: "I know that Messias cometh, which is called Christ: when he is come, he will tell us all things." This woman with whom Jesus talks at the well of Sychar is, however, a woman of soiled life. At one time or another she has lived with five different men, and the man with whom she is now living is not her husband. This is the woman to whom Jesus offers the water of life.

It is obvious that when Jesus makes His offer He is using the symbolism of water to give expression to His claim that He can satisfy the deepest spiritual needs of the woman. The need for water is common to all mankind. When we live in a land where there is an abundance of water we forget this need, but the woman of Samaria was quite familiar with it. She had to make the journey from her home to the well every day to draw water. She was weary of this toil and she sought release from it. Jesus is using the thirst of the body for water to describe those deeper cravings which are common to all mankind. We think, for example, of the desire for the knowledge of the meaning and purpose of our human existence, or of the yearning of man the creature for some knowledge of his Creator. Jesus tells this woman that He can permanently satisfy the deepest cravings of her spiritual life. He offers to give her the water that shall be in her "a well of water springing up into everlasting life."

To make it possible for the woman to believe in Him, He gives her a sign: He reveals to her the knowledge which He, a stranger, has of the intimate affairs of her personal life. It is this sign which leads her to the conviction that He is the Christ. She says to her people: "Come, see a man, which told me all things that ever I did: is not this the Christ?" (John 4:29.) To this woman Jesus makes the clear and unqualified statement that He is the Christ. When she refers to the coming Messiah, Jesus says to her: "I that speak unto thee am he." (John 4:26.) This statement is unique. John gives us in successive interviews the reactions of various people who come into contact with Jesus. Many of them recognize Him as the Christ. Jesus does not rebuke them. He never denies Himself, but when He moves among the Jews He does not proclaim Himself as the Christ.

The difference between the Gospel of John and the first three Gospels should not be magnified. In the other Gospels also people wonder if Jesus is the Messiah, and here also Jesus never denies that He is the Christ. In the scene at Caesarea Philippi, which probably comes about six months before the end of His ministry, Jesus accepts Peter's recognition of Him as the Christ; but He immediately proceeds to identify the idea of the Christ with that of the Suffering Servant. And He charges His disciples not to proclaim Him as the Christ. (Matthew 16:20.) While Jesus does not give His reasons, we believe that the reserve with which He uses this title among His own people is related to the distortion of the idea of the Christ which prevailed among the Jews. Jesus was the Christ, but He was not the kind of Christ that the Jews were expecting. Among the Samaritans the concept of the Christ had not been corrupted by Jewish nationalism. This may be the reason why Jesus does not hesitate to tell the woman of Samaria that He is the Christ. In Mark's account of the trial before Pilate, Jesus also affirms that He is the Messiah; but at this stage He would hardly be misunderstood since He was entering upon the fulfillment of the concept of the Suffering Servant.

The revelation of Himself to the woman of Samaria as the Christ is in confirmation of the teaching about the nature of God which He has given to her. In her effort to avoid the disclosure which Jesus has made to her of His knowledge of her sin and guilt, she says to Him: "Our fathers worshipped in this mountain; and ye say, that in Jerusalem is the place where men ought to worship." She refers to the centuries-old debate between the Jews and the Samaritans over the proper place to worship God. Jesus says to her: "Woman, believe me, the hour cometh, when ye shall neither in this mountain, nor yet at Jerusalem, worship the Father. Ye worship ye know not what: we know what we worship: for salvation is of the Jews. But the hour cometh, and now is, when the true worshippers shall worship the Father in spirit and in truth: for the Father seeketh such to worship him. God is a Spirit: and they that worship him must worship him in spirit and in truth." (John 4:21-24.)

Jesus reminds this woman that God is a Spirit. He says this in answer to her question about the place of worship. God is a Spirit. He does not have a body like men; and because He does not have a body He is not localized. To find a man we have to go where the man is. But God is a Spirit. As eternal Spirit He is omnipresent. We do not have to go to some specified spot to find God. He is spiritually present with His people wherever they draw near to Him in spirit and in truth.

When Jesus said, "God is a Spirit," He opposed all efforts to localize God. But He went further and declared that God is a Spirit even as we are spirits. We draw close to His meaning when we say that God is a Person. He is a being who has the power to think, and feel, and act. When the human creature stands before his Creator, an *I* confronts a *Thou*. The God who comes to us in Christ is not an impersonal force. He is not a cosmic urge or an evolutionary hypothesis. He is a Spirit. We are embodied spirits. He is pure Spirit. We cannot conceive of pure Spirit, but we can believe that our Creator is a Person.

Jesus goes further and gives the conditions of worship. He says that those who worship the Father must worship Him in *spirit* and in truth. When Jesus says that we must worship in spirit, He means that the fundamental thing in worship is the attitude of our human spirits in the presence of the eternal Spirit. Whether we are in Samaria or in Jerusalem is not important. The crucial question deals with our own spiritual attitudes. God resists the proud and gives grace to the humble. He gives Himself to those who respond to Him in love and obedience. The vision of God is given to the pure in heart.

Jesus says also that we must worship in *truth*. By this He does not mean that worship must be genuine. The need for sincerity can be taken for granted. But Jesus is insisting here that our worship of God must be based on a correct knowledge of His character and His will for us. This is the fatal flaw in Samaritan worship. The religion of the Samaritans was a syncretism of pagan and Jewish elements. Jesus could say to the woman of Samaria: "Ye worship ye know not what: we know what we worship: for salvation is of the Jews." (John 4:22.) Evidently the concept of God which this woman worshiped had not made excessive moral demands on her life. The desire for worship is not enough. We must know the true character of God. We must know the duty which He requires of us. In this argument, Jesus definitely takes the side of the Jews. The knowledge of God has come to us through His revelation of Himself to Israel. We would carry this argument a step further if we said that the final revelation of God is in the face of the Christ. God spoke to the fathers through the prophets, but He has spoken unto us through His Son. (Hebrews 1:1-2.)

Jesus reveals to the woman of Samaria the Father who *seeks* for those who will worship Him in spirit and in truth. The God of the universe is not some distant deity who does not know or care about us. He is the God and Father of our Lord Jesus Christ, who is concerned that each of us shall worship Him in spirit and in truth. Jesus reveals the seeking Father through the three parables in Luke 15. The woman seeks her lost coin. The shepherd seeks his lost sheep. The father seeks his lost boy. The full revelation of the seeking father is given in the coming of Jesus. God loves us and sends His Son to die for us. He seeks to enable us to realize our best selves through worship. Jesus came from the seeking Father. He finds the woman of Samaria. He tells her that if she had known who was speaking unto her she would have asked of Him and *He* would have given her living water. He insists that if she had asked for the living water *He* would have given it to her. This is His assertion that He can satisfy her deepest needs in this life and can lead her to the life which is eternal. He continues to offer the living water to those who will ask for it.

"The publicans and the harlots go into the kingdom of God before you."—Matthew 21:31.

11. SIMON THE PHARISEE

Scripture background: Luke 7:36-50.

Simon the Pharisee invited Jesus to have dinner with him. We do not know why Simon issued this invitation. He probably had heard Jesus preach and wanted to have a personal contact with Him. He may have been interested in deciding whether or not the Prophet from Nazareth was a teacher of religion whom he could support. Jesus accepted the invitation, but Simon was somewhat condescending in his attitude toward Him. When Jesus entered his home Simon did not give Him the customary kiss of greeting. And he did not have on hand the bowl of water in which a guest was expected to bathe his feet after removing his sandals and before entering the home.

In an Oriental home of the first century, it was customary for the guests to recline on couches. The meal was probably served in a number of courses and was expected to last for several hours.

It afforded an opportunity both for food and for extended conversation. Often those who were not invited to the dinner were permitted to enter the room and listen to the conversation.

At some time during this meal a woman entered the hall who was certainly not one of the invited guests. Simon recognized her at once as a woman who was a sinner. He knew that she had been a woman of the streets. The woman approached Jesus as He was lying on the couch with His feet toward her. She had in her hand an alabaster box of ointment. As she stood beside Jesus she burst into tears, and the tears fell on His feet. She stooped and dried His feet with her hair. Then she proceeded to anoint them with the ointment which she had brought and to kiss them.

We must not avoid the facts concerning this woman. Simon knew her reputation, and Jesus Himself said that her sins were many. This woman had sold herself for hire. She had misused her womanhood, flaunting the moral order as expressed in the seventh commandment. Her cup of iniquity was full. Simon expressed the judgment of society when he felt that such a woman should be shunned. A respectable society has to protect itself by casting out those who have violated its moral standards.

Why, then, did this woman enter the home of Simon the Pharisee? We can be sure that before her coming she had heard Jesus preach. She must have heard Him declare that God was ready to forgive all those who would turn to Him in repentance, faith, and new obedience. She believed that Jesus was One who had come to seek and save the lost. She knew that He was interested in her, that He loved her. This encounter with Jesus reawakened her conscience. It gave her a sense of her sin over against the holiness of God as seen in Jesus Christ. Jesus called this woman back to her true self. He gave her hope in God's forgiveness. In response to the message which she had received through Jesus this woman surrendered her life to God and received forgiveness, the removal of guilt, the sense of cleansing. When she entered the home of Simon the Pharisee she was a changed person, but she still had the difficult task of re-establishing herself in the society that had cast her out.

She came to Jesus in the home of Simon because she had an

overwhelming desire to reveal her love to the One who had saved her from her sins. The depth of her love is shown in her willingness to face the criticism of the Pharisees. Jesus accepted her devotion. He did not rebuke her as she stooped and kissed His feet.

As Simon observed the attitude of Jesus toward this woman he said to himself, "This man, if he were a prophet, would have known who and what manner of woman this is that toucheth him: for she is a sinner." (Luke 7:39.) Simon felt that the failure of Jesus to rebuke this woman was proof that He was not a true prophet. In answer to Simon's unspoken thoughts Jesus tells the parable of the two debtors. One had owed fifty pence, the other five hundred. Neither had been able to pay, and the creditor had forgiven them both. It is Simon who says that the one who had been forgiven the most would love the most. As we consider this parable in its setting it is obvious that Jesus in His description of the two debtors refers to Simon and the woman. He realizes that this woman has been a great sinner, and He estimates her debt as ten times that of Simon. But neither debtor is able to pay. Simon the Pharisee and the woman of the street must both enter the Kingdom by the road of repentance and forgiveness. To the self-righteous Pharisee, the last word of insult comes when the righteousness he presents to God is rejected and the Son of God can do nothing for him but die for his sins. At times the Pharisee finds it more difficult than the harlot to understand the meaning of a salvation that is based on grace alone.

Jesus proceeds to contrast Simon and the woman of the street. The contrast, of course, is not between Simon and the woman in the days of her shame. The contrast is between Simon and the woman as she kneels penitent and contrite at the feet of Jesus. To Simon's horror, Jesus finds that this woman compares favorably with Simon. Her love for Jesus is greater than his love. The unnamed woman has brought to Jesus a depth of devotion which is quite unknown to Simon. She has expressed this devotion through her purchase of the precious ointment with which she anoints the feet of Jesus. She knows a love that does not count the cost. She has been so overcome with her emotion that she has not been able to control her tears. Simon is a stranger to any such emotion. We do not have to experience the depths of iniquity to know the love of Jesus. Paul knew that the Son of God loved him and had given Himself for him. When Jesus came to seek and save the lost He went to the final limits of love. He loved His own and He loved them to the end. As we think of Him who loved us and gave Himself for us we should find that His love calls forth our full devotion.

The woman was superior to Simon in the area of faith. Simon is about to decide that Jesus is not even a true prophet, but this woman has found in Him the Saviour from sin. She has believed His message and accepted the forgiveness of God which He has offered. Simon is making a decision concerning Jesus, and in so doing he is revealing himself. We have here the beginning of that opposition of the Pharisees which is to harden rapidly into unbelief. Simon cannot understand Jesus' attitude toward publicans and harlots. If Simon continues in this attitude he will in time join those who seek to destroy Jesus. The simple truth is that the harlot has found her way into the Kingdom of God which Simon the Pharisee has refused to enter.

The attitude of Jesus which is revealed here became an outstanding characteristic of the Church which He founded. "Ancient critics lashed at the Church for its foolish unconcern with what people had been before they came to Christ. Celsus wrote that other religious leaders called the clean and intellectual, the pure and honorable to become their followers. But this Christ, said Celsus, invites sinners, foolish, simple-minded, the unfortunate. 'Why, if you wanted an assembly of robbers, these are just the sort of people you would summon!' And the Church, instead of cringing under the blows, exulted: 'Yes! Out of those that others would throw on the trash heap, Christ has made and does make men who are clean and pure and Christlike!' A great church historian, Harnack, remarks, 'Celsus has stated as lucidly as one could desire the cardinal difference between Christianity and ancient religions.' "*

* Connolly Gamble, *Senior Teacher's Guide*, January-March, 1958, Presbyterian Graded Series, pp. 24-25. Richmond, Va.: Board of Christian Education, Presbyterian Church, U. S.

On another occasion Jesus said to the chief priests and the elders of the people: "Verily I say unto you, That the publicans and the harlots go into the kingdom of God before you." (Matthew 21:31.) There is much that can be said for Simon, but the central message of the story is that his trust in his own righteousness prevented him from finding his way into the Kingdom of God. Jesus offers to all a forgiveness based on the grace of God. And all men must enter this Kingdom as they receive the righteousness which comes by grace alone through faith alone.

"This day is salvation come to this house."—Luke 19:9.

12. ZACCHAEUS

Scripture background: Luke 19:1-10.

Zacchaeus was a Jew. As a Jew he was rooted in the whole story of the Messianic nation called to be the instrument of God's redemptive purpose in the world. But Zacchaeus was not worthy of his heritage as a son of Abraham. He was a publican. He had departed so far from his spiritual heritage that he was cast out by the Judaism of his time. He had sold himself to the Romans to collect taxes from his own people. In this business of playing traitor to his people he had risen to the top; he was known as a chief publican. And he had become rich. We are probably well within the facts when we suggest that he had used his power as a chief publican not only to collect taxes for the Romans but also to amass a fortune for himself at the expense of his own people. The Pharisee in the parable of the Pharisee and the publican could insist that he was not an extortioner. The idea was probably suggested to him by the presence of the publican. The besetting sin of the publicans was extortion. It was probably by this means that Zacchaeus had grown rich.

Since he was protected by the Roman power, the people of Jericho had to tolerate Zacchaeus. But Jewish society could avenge itself on the publicans by making them outcasts from respectable society. Zacchaeus was such an outcast. He was no longer treated by his own people as a son of Abraham. When we add to this description the knowledge that Zacchaeus was short of stature, we have our picture of the man who was despised and feared in Jericho.

Zacchaeus met Jesus. There is much human interest in the story of the little man who sees a crowd moving through the streets of Jericho and seeks to get through the crowd to find the man at the center of it. The person who is short of stature is at a great disadvantage in a crowd. He cannot see over the heads of other men, and he cannot push through to the center. Anyone who has watched crowds has seen the predicament of the little man who needs someone to lift him up so that he can see.

Zacchaeus solved his problem by going ahead of the crowd and climbing a sycamore tree and waiting for the procession to pass beneath him. He was in that tree to satisfy his curiosity. He wanted to see who was causing the commotion. The probability is that he already had some knowledge of this man. Jesus' ministry was not carried on in a corner, and this meeting with Zacchaeus took place just before the beginning of Passion Week, as Jesus was on His last trip to Jerusalem. Zacchaeus may have known of Jesus as teacher and healer. He may also have heard that Jesus was known as the friend of publicans and sinners. Thoughts like these may have run through his mind as the crowd moved toward him and he saw that the Prophet from Nazareth was at its center.

But Zacchaeus was probably not prepared for the way Jesus greeted him. When Jesus came to where Zacchaeus was, He looked up at him and said: "Zacchaeus, make haste, and come down; for to day I must abide at thy house." In saying this, Jesus deliberately cut across the established social customs of His time. In all societies the eating of a meal with a man is a symbol of social equality. In announcing that He wished to be Zacchaeus' guest, Jesus was seeking to win Zacchaeus at the expense of violating the caste system of Jewish society. We realize the force of this when we are told that all the people murmured, saying: "He is gone in to lodge with a man that is a sinner." (Luke 19:7, A.S.V.) Zacchaeus responded at once to the word of Jesus to him. He made haste and came down and received Him joyfully.

Jesus went home with Zacchaeus. We do not know how long He stayed. He may have spent part of a day. It is possible that He spent the night and that the scene which is described for us in verses 8-10 took place the next day. The important thing to remember is that Jesus sat down in Zacchaeus' home and talked with him about his spiritual welfare. We do not know all that Jesus said to Zacchaeus, but the story itself gives us some suggestions about what must have taken place in the conversation between the Prophet from Nazareth and the chief publican of Jericho. Jesus reminded Zacchaeus of his spiritual heritage as a son of Abraham. In this He emphasized not the distorted idea of a son of Abraham which prevailed among the Jews, but the spiritual heritage which Zacchaeus could have as a member of the Israel of God. Like the prodigal in the far country, Zacchaeus was given again the vision of the Father's home, the knowledge of the heritage which he had defiled.

Jesus offered Zacchaeus the forgiveness of God. He Himself makes the statement: "To-day is salvation come to this house." The terms upon which Jesus offered this salvation are not stated in this story, but they cannot have been out of harmony with the central theme of His message. He called all men to repent and to believe the goods news of the Kingdom of God. He required of Zacchaeus repentance (the acknowledgment of the evil of his life), faith (a renewed trust in God), and obedience (the surrender to the rule of God in his life).

Jesus told Zacchaeus that genuine repentance would involve the effort to go back into his past and seek so far as possible to right the wrongs he had done. The willingness to make restitution is often the test of the genuineness of repentance. After his conscience has been awakened by the play which Hamlet has had performed before him, the king in Shakespeare's tragedy finds that he cannot pray, "Forgive me my foul murder." He continues:

> "That cannot be; since I am still possess'd
> Of those effects for which I did the murder,
> My crown, mine own ambition, and my queen."*

* William Shakespeare, *Hamlet*. Act III, scene iii, lines 52-55.

Jesus made it clear to Zacchaeus that genuine repentance would be a very costly affair. He may have suggested that Zacchaeus dedicate a portion of his remaining wealth to the ministry to the poor. (It is interesting to notice that He asks the rich young ruler to sell all that he has and give to the poor but accepts the offer of Zacchaeus to give the half of his goods. This shows that the demand made on the young ruler was a test of his loyalty and not a regular requirement of discipleship.)

Jesus challenged Zacchaeus to be worthy of his heritage. Zacchaeus responded to Him in faith and obedience as a child of God, and Jesus declared that salvation had come to the home of Zacchaeus. As He offers forgiveness, Jesus says: "The Son of man came to seek and to save that which was lost." (Luke 19:10, A.S.V.) The seeking of Zacchaeus is an expression of the central purpose of Jesus in the days of His flesh. He was interested in publicans and sinners because He had come to seek and to save the lost. A short time before this He told the parable of the seeking shepherd who left the ninety and nine to find one lost sheep. We have here a picture of the Saviour who seeks and finds one lost man and restores him to his rightful place as a son of Abraham. The risen Lord is still the seeking Christ who offers us His forgiveness and seeks to bring us into the Kingdom of God.

Jesus as Saviour reveals the heart of the eternal God. God was in Christ reconciling the world unto Himself. The Father comes to us through the Son. As Jesus seeks for the soul of Zacchaeus we have a revelation of the Father who so loved the world that He sent His only begotten Son that whosoever believes on Him should not perish but should have everlasting life.

"I also am a man under authority."—Matthew 8:9, A.S.V.

13. A CENTURION FROM CAPERNAUM

Scripture background: Matthew 8:5-13; Luke 7:1-10.

The story of the healing of the centurion's servant has been preserved for us in two forms. In Matthew the Roman centurion comes to Capernaum and deals directly with Jesus. In Luke he sends messengers to Jesus but does not come himself. Luke tells us that the centurion had built a synagogue for the Jews in Capernaum. Matthew gives us in verse 11 a saying of Jesus concerning those who will come from the east and the west to sit down in the Kingdom of heaven. Luke, with his tremendous interest in the spread of Christianity to the Gentiles, would hardly have omitted this verse if it had been in his sources. These differences in detail do not affect the central point of the story. They do show that the power of Scripture to become the word of God to us is not dependent on its complete agreement in the details.

This story centers around a Roman centurion who lived in Capernaum. He was an officer in the army of occupation. Usually such men were not beloved, but this centurion had become deeply interested in the Jewish people. He had probably found in Judaism a knowledge of God which was not to be found in paganism. He found also a moral code based on the Ten Commandments which was far more exalted than the ethical codes of the Graeco-Roman world. The centurion's interest in the religion of the Jews had gone so deep that he had built a synagogue at Capernaum. The Jews could say of him: "He loveth our nation." (Luke 7:5.) This is an unusual tribute for a conquered people to pay to an officer in the army of a conquering power.

A servant of the centurion was seriously ill. Matthew tells us that he was "sick of the palsy, grievously tormented." Luke says that he was "sick, and ready to die." With genuine compassion the Roman officer sought aid for his servant. He had heard of the miracles of healing performed in Capernaum by the young teacher from Nazareth. He wanted Jesus to come and heal his servant.

But the centurion faced a deeply rooted custom of the Jews. An orthodox Jew was not supposed to enter the home of a Gentile. This custom was based on the ideas of clean and unclean. A Jew who entered the home of a Gentile was thought to have become ceremonially unclean. The emphasis on the custom had been developed in an effort to keep the Jews a separate people in the midst of their Gentile neighbors. Regardless of its origin, this practice was one about which Jesus' contemporaries felt quite keenly. When Peter a few years later in Caesarea entered the home of a Roman centurion named Cornelius, he was met on his return to Jerusalem with the words: "Thou wentest in to men uncircumcised, and didst eat with them." (Acts 11:3.) This violation of established custom seemed even to the Christian Jews more important than the story of the conversion of Cornelius and his household.

Jesus lived under the law. He observed the law as part of the habits of His life, but He was not too deeply concerned about violating the ceremonial laws of clean and unclean. He was prepared to go at once to the centurion's home and heal his servant. But the centurion, who knew and loved the Jews, knew also how the contemporaries of Jesus would feel about His entering the home of a Gentile. With a fine respect for the feelings of Jesus, he does not want to ask Him to do something that he knows the leaders of the Jews will condemn. In a similar way a Negro minister today might hesitate to visit the home of his white friend for fear of leading the white man to a violation of social custom which his associates might condemn.

The centurion had in his own life an experience which gave him something of an understanding of Jesus. He himself was a man who had been set under orders. There is a vast difference between a man with authority and a man who is under orders. This man was a part of the military discipline of Rome. If he had received an order to gather together his command and march to Parthia, he would have obeyed without question. He took his orders from Rome and obeyed them, and in handling his own men this officer of Rome was accustomed to expect and receive obedience. He says: "I say to this man, Go, and he goeth; and to another, Come, and he cometh; and to my servant, Do this, and he doeth it." (Matthew 8:9.) There is an intimate relation between this man's being under orders and his capacity to get obedience from his men. The Romans used to say that no man was competent to command until he had first learned to obey. If the centurion had ordered his company to Parthia he would not have been acting on his own caprice. He would have moved in obedience to a command he had received. And, if he had needed it, all the power of Rome would have been available to enforce his orders.

Against the background of his own experience of being a man under orders, the centurion came to a deeper understanding of Jesus. He said to Jesus: "I *also* am a man under authority." (Matthew 8:9, A.S.V.) He felt instinctively that Jesus was a man under authority. Jesus had come because the Father had sent Him. The centurion was under the authority of Rome. Jesus came in obedience to the will of God. The centurion felt that the secret of the power of God which was being released through Jesus was the obedience of Jesus to the will of God.

As the centurion thought of the relation of Jesus to God, he found a solution to his dilemma. He decided that it was not necessary for Jesus to come to his home in order to heal his servant. He was confident that if Jesus would speak the word, the power of God would be released and his servant would be healed.

Jesus was amazed at the faith of this man who stood outside the community of Israel. He said of him: "I have not found so great faith, no, not in Israel." (Matthew 8:10.) As Jesus thinks of the Roman soldier He sees in him a symbol of the mighty multitude which shall ultimately come into the Kingdom of God from those who do not come from the children of Abraham according to the flesh. He says: "I say unto you, That many shall come from the east and west, and shall sit down with Abraham, and Isaac, and Jacob, in the kingdom of heaven." (Matthew 8:11.) As we think of these words in their setting we cannot fail to see in them a reference to Jewish exclusiveness expressed in the unwillingness of the Jews even to enter a home of the Gentiles. Jesus says that many shall come from the east and west and shall sit down with Abraham and Isaac and Jacob in the Kingdom of heaven. The darker side of the picture follows; Jesus says: "But the children of the kingdom shall be cast out into outer darkness: there shall be weeping and gnashing of teeth." (Matthew 8:12.) When we refuse to receive into the fellowship of the Church people of other races and nations we may act in such a manner that we exclude ourselves from the Kingdom of heaven. The privileged people of our contemporary society may some day realize that they have proved unworthy of the Kingdom and that Jesus has gathered into His Kingdom those whom they have considered inferior, and has made them the instruments of His purpose.

The Roman centurion understood that Jesus was a man under authority. He could understand Jesus because he himself knew both how to obey and how to command. In a similar way Jesus expects those who follow Him to be under His orders. There is in the heart of each of us a deep craving to find the meaning of our existence in something that is bigger and greater than we are. One person expressed this by saying: "I want to find a person strong enough to master me and great enough and good enough that I can find the fulfillment of my life in surrender to him." It is tragic if in our yearning for authority we give ourselves in complete obedience to someone who betrays us. A dictator may ask for the allegiance of his people. In the end he may betray their trust and lead them in the way of destruction. But Jesus is strong enough to master us and great and good enough for us to find the fulfillment of life in His service. Jesus comes to us in humility. He is willing to wash the feet of His disciples, but there must be no doubt about who is Master. He says to them: "Ye call me Master and Lord: and ye say well; for so I am." (John 13:13.)

The centurion could command because he was under orders. He could call on resources of power because he was in obedience to Rome. In a similar way, the power of Jesus is released through those who move in obedience to His commands. The Christian is not free to do as he pleases. He has voluntarily placed himself under orders. He acknowledges Jesus as his Lord and Master. He seeks to live in a way that is pleasing to Him. We cannot use Jesus. We cannot manipulate Him. But we can serve Him. Those who acknowledge Him as Lord and move out in obedience to Him can become the instruments of His power.

"*. . . and fell down on his face at his feet, giving him thanks: and he was a Samaritan.*"—*Luke 17:16.*

14. THE SAMARITAN WHO GAVE THANKS

Scripture background: Luke 17:11-19.

As Jesus was passing along the border between Samaria and Galilee on His way to Jerusalem, He was met by ten lepers. The leper was a familiar sight in the ancient East. Because of fear of the contagion of leprosy, those who were afflicted with this disease were immediately isolated from all who were not leprous. We know today that leprosy is no more contagious than many other diseases, but the fear remains with us. Those who have contracted the disease cannot move in the normal contacts of life. One of the most moving books of our time, entitled *Who Walk Alone*, was written by Percy Burgess and published in 1940. It is the story of an American soldier who contracted leprosy during the Spanish-American War and found it necessary to spend the rest of his life in a leper colony in the Philippines.

Because lepers in Jesus' day were isolated from all other people, they often gathered together in bands and carried on a limited type of communal life. In this band of ten lepers, there was one man who was a Samaritan. The deep-seated line of division between Jews and Samaritans disappeared in the common tragedy of disease and isolation. Why should men worry about the shades of religious belief and the peculiarities of racial inheritance when they were all forced by their disease to be separated from the society which had nurtured them?

Because the lepers could not mingle with other people, they were cut off from the normal means of making a living. This meant that many of them were reduced to begging. They were dependent on the charity of others. Leprosy was usually considered incurable, but at times a sore which had been thought to be leprous did heal. In this case, the man who had reason to think that the diagnosis of his case was wrong could present himself to the priest for examination. (Leviticus 14:2.) If the priest pronounced him clean, he was permitted to return to his normal life.

While leprosy was usually considered incurable, hope had begun to stir among the lepers of Palestine. They had heard of the appearance of a Preacher and Healer named Jesus of Nazareth who had been successful in His healing of lepers. In the message which He sends to the doubting John, Jesus lists among other signs the fact that "the lepers are cleansed." (Luke 7:22. See Matthew 8:2; Mark 1:40; Luke 5:12.) The evangelists record several specific incidents in which those afflicted with leprosy are healed. With a hope born of the reports which had reached them, the ten lepers came to Jesus. They stood afar off, as they usually were not permitted to come close to those who were not lepers, and they cried out: "Jesus, Master, have mercy on us."

The ear of Jesus was always attuned to the call of need. He heard their cry and said to them: "Go show yourselves unto the priests." This must have seemed at first a strange command. Lepers went to the priests after they were healed, not before. But perhaps as they talked together they remembered the advice given by his counselors to Naaman, the leper. Elisha said to him: "Go and wash in Jordan seven times, and thy flesh shall come again to thee, and thou shalt be clean." (2 Kings 5:10.) His servants said to him: "My father, if the prophet had bid thee do some great thing, wouldest thou not have done it? How much rather then, when he saith to thee, Wash, and be clean?" (2 Kings 5:13.) The lepers had nothing to lose and everything to gain. In obedience, they started out on the journey to the priest.

They may have gone for some distance before they were conscious of any change in their condition, but at some point in their journey they were cleansed. Who can describe the joy of these men as they suddenly became aware of their deliverance. They hastened to the priest with quickened steps; that is, nine of them did. But the one who was a Samaritan stopped dead in his tracks; and then, forsaking his companions, he retraced his steps until he found Jesus. He fell prostrate at the Master's feet, giving Him thanks and glorifying God. Jesus looked upon him and said: "Were there not ten cleansed? but where are the nine? There are not found that returned to give glory to God, save this stranger." And he said to the man: "Arise, go thy way: thy faith hath made thee whole."

The man who came back received a spiritual blessing. The words, "thy faith hath made thee whole," refer first of all to the miracle of cleansing which the man had experienced. Jesus says the same thing on other occasions to those who were healed by Him. Consider, for example, the woman with an issue of blood. (Matthew 9:22.) In the miracles of healing, there was need for co-operation between the patient and the healer. If the lepers had not had enough faith to start on the journey to the priests, they would not have been healed. The power of God which was available in Jesus Christ was released as men acted in faith.

The principles illustrated here in the healing of the body are also valid in Jesus' ministry to the souls of men. We must respond with faith in what Jesus says to us. The man who returned to give thanks renewed his contact with Jesus. We can be reasonably sure that he became one of His followers. As a disciple of Jesus he would experience the deepest satisfactions of this life, and he would lay hold of the hope of the eternal life.

Jesus looks upon the Samaritan and asks: "Where are the nine?" His concern is with the men who did not return to give glory to God. It is hard to understand the failure of these men to take time to return and thank the man who had healed them. We often fail to appreciate the blessings of life until we lose them, but these lepers had known sickness, and isolation, and despair. Then they had been suddenly and miraculously cured. Surely their hearts must have been filled with a sense of thanksgiving for their deliverance. Perhaps they intended to express their gratitude after they had been pronounced clean by the priest, but if they did, they never translated these intentions into actions. How often in similar cases men have neglected the obligation to express their thanks until the sense of gratitude has gone out of their hearts!

The nine who were healed cannot have failed to experience the joy of restoration to health, and with this joy there must have been a sense of gratitude to Jesus as their healer. But they may have reasoned that it was unnecessary to go to the inconvenience of a trip back to express their gratitude. They may have said to each other that Jesus knew they were healed and knew also that they were grateful. It is more important for us to feel gratitude than it is for us to express it. Certainly we do not want to go through the form of expressing it when we do not feel it, but the emotion which is never expressed soon disappears. The Samaritan who returned must have found in his gratitude for what Jesus had done a deep motivation for righteous living in the days to come. The gratitude of the nine who did not come back was probably a fleeting experience which did not permanently affect their lives.

The sin of ingratitude roots in selfishness. If we are centered in ourselves, we do not like to be under obligation to others. We can become so selfish that we lose our capacity to feel gratitude. We can let ourselves get into an attitude of mind in which we accept with no sense of gratitude all that is done for us. Here again sin defeats itself. Those who minister to us will find it hard to continue if their best efforts remain unappreciated. The sin of ingratitude can prepare the way for spiritual deterioration. When Paul describes the moral breakdown of mankind in the first chapter of Romans, he says that those who knew God did not glorify Him as God and were not thankful. He goes on to say that they became vain in their imaginations and that their foolish hearts were darkened. (Romans 1:21.)

We have been thinking of the one man who came back and of the nine who did not return to give thanks. We need to consider also the picture of Jesus which is given us in this story. His heart was moved with a deep sense of satisfaction when the Samaritan fell at His feet and gave Him thanks. There is a note of wistfulness in His voice as He says: "Were there not ten cleansed? but where are the nine?" Jesus did not perform His mighty works to win the praises of men. He moved through life in obedience to His Father's will. He sought always to do what was pleasing to the Father. His miracles of healing were an expression of His compassion. He could carry on His ministry with or without the appreciation of those to whom He ministered, but His heart was encouraged when men gave Him their devotion. He carried on a daily ministry to others in which strength went out of Him. His spirit was lifted when His ministry was received with appreciation, and the ingratitude of men as revealed in the attitude of the nine who did not return to give glory to God weighed upon Him. Jesus speaks here for those who minister in His name. The servant of Jesus does not condition His ministry on the way in which it is received. The missionary may be willing to sow the seed and wait many years for the harvest to come in; but he does want to know that his message has been received and understood, and he feels keenly the ingratitude of those who accept his ministry and never take time to say thank you.

Jesus reveals also the heart of God. The attitudes of Jesus in the context of our earthly life are a disclosure of the heart of the Father in heaven. When Jesus responds to the gratitude of the Samaritan we remember that He has told us of the joy there is in heaven over one sinner who repents. And as Jesus asks, "Where are the nine?" we feel the sorrow that is at the heart of God when His children on earth do not lift their hearts in thanksgiving to Him. Isaiah, in his fifth chapter, tells the story of the vineyard which should have borne good grapes but instead has produced wild grapes. He points his story as he says: "The vineyard of the

Lord of hosts is the house of Israel, and the men of Judah his pleasant plant: and he looked for judgment, but behold oppression; for righteousness, but behold a cry." (Isaiah 5:7.) The heart of the eternal God is grieved by man's ingratitude.

"How hard is it for them that trust in riches to enter into the kingdom of God!"—Mark 10:24.

15. THE RICH YOUNG RULER

Scripture background: Matthew 19:16-30; Mark 10:17-31; Luke 18:18-30.

The rich young ruler presents one of the most attractive and at the same time one of the most tragic of the faces about the Christ. He is usually thought of as a young man. The evangelists do not say he was young, but they do say that he came running. Only the young are apt to come running. Yet this man tells Jesus that he has kept the commandments from his youth up. This would indicate that he had some maturity. He was young enough to run but old enough to look back upon his youth. He was probably a man at the peak of his powers.

Luke tells us that the man was a ruler. We do not know the full meaning of the statement. He may have been a ruler of the synagogue. He may have been a man of royal blood who ruled over a great estate. We can be sure that he belonged to the nobility and that he had all the prestige and influence which go with high position.

All the evangelists say that he was rich. Matthew and Mark say "he had great possessions," and Luke says that he was "very rich." No suggestion is given about how he became rich. There is no indication of dishonesty in the accumulation of his wealth. He had kept the commandments. As far as we know he had not grown rich by extortion or oppression. Probably he had inherited his money. We do know that when the ruler came to Jesus he was recognized at once as a man of great wealth. Wealth is stored-up human energy. The control of great wealth is also the control of great power.

The man who comes to Jesus has youth, and position, and wealth. These are things that are more or less external, but this man has also qualities of the spirit which commend him. He comes running. This may be a sign of youth. It is also a sign of eagerness. We do not know why he came running. He may have debated within himself the wisdom of coming to Jesus. It was somewhat unusual for a man of his position and influence to come openly to the Prophet from Nazareth. Nicodemus had preferred to come in the night. But when the ruler decides to come he comes openly in a way that is certain to attract attention. There must have been eagerness and expectancy in his face as he came running to Jesus.

When the ruler reached Jesus he knelt as he asked his question. This indicates humility of spirit. He belongs to the rich and the powerful, but he is humble in the presence of the Teacher who had been a carpenter of Nazareth. He does not show the arrogance of wealth or the pride of position.

The young ruler was a man of integrity. When Jesus tells him to keep the commandments, he replies: "Master, all these have I observed from my youth." And Mark adds: "Then Jesus beholding him loved him." (Mark 10:20-21.) We can properly raise questions concerning the extent to which it is possible for any man to keep satisfactorily the commandments of God, but there is no question about the sincerity of this answer. Mark would not have said that Jesus looked upon him and loved him if the answer had not been genuine. As a boy the young ruler had been taught the Ten Commandments. He had accepted them as binding upon him. To the best of his ability he had kept them. This means that he was free from profanity, impurity, and dishonesty. He shared with his people their respect for the Sabbath, their hatred of idolatry, and their devotion to the God of Israel.

Why did this ruler come to Jesus? He came to find the answer to a question. His question was: "Good Master, what shall I do that I may inherit eternal life?" As a rich man he had the leisure that goes with wealth. He had time to reflect on the meaning and purpose of life. He knew as all men know that our human life is marked by existence unto death. He had youth and position and wealth, but he was aware of the truth that Gray expressed so beautifully for us when he said:

> "The boast of heraldry, the pomp of power,
> And all that beauty, all that wealth e'er gave,
> Await alike th' inevitable hour:—
> The paths of glory lead but to the grave.*

The ruler may have heard Jesus tell the story of the rich fool who laid up treasure for himself and was not rich toward God. Perhaps Jesus' question, "Then whose shall those things be?" (Luke 12:20), was with him as he surveyed his great possessions.

The question which he brings to Jesus is one of the great questions. It is a question which concerns us all. We know that the grave is certain. If there is a life beyond the grave we want to know about it, and if it is possible within this life to inherit eternal life we want to know how. The way in which the ruler put his question is somewhat interesting. He says: *What shall I do that I may inherit eternal life?"* He is thinking in terms of work righteousness. He does not know that the bestowal of eternal life is the gracious gift of God.

Why did this man come to *Jesus* with this question? The answer is that he must have felt that Jesus had the secret of eternal life. He may have heard Jesus preach; and he must have felt that there was about Jesus a quality of life which he did not have. The ruler and Jesus stand in strong contrast. He has great possessions and Jesus can say of Himself that "the foxes have holes, and the birds of the air have nests; but the Son of man hath not where to lay his head." (Matthew 8:20.) But if Jesus has the secret of eternal life He is richer than the ruler. It was Jesus who asked the question, "What shall it profit a man, if he shall gain the whole world, and lose his own soul?" (Mark 8:36.)

Jesus' first answer must have been disappointing to the young ruler, who probably expected a unique and unusual reply to his question. Jesus says to him: "If thou wilt enter into life, keep the

* Thomas Gray, "Elegy Written in a Country Churchyard," lines 33-36.

commandments." Jesus then proceeds to summarize for him the second part of the decalogue. He adds the commandment: "Thou shalt love thy neighbor as thyself." Jesus does not abolish the commandments. He reaffirms them. He deepens them by moving from a righteousness of external act to a righteousness of inner thought and motive. The law condemns adultery. Jesus condemns the man who looks upon a woman to lust after her. The law condemns murder. Jesus deals with the hate which leads to murder. The law itself moves into this area when it condemns covetousness. It deals here with motive rather than deed. If we interpret obedience to the commandments merely in terms of not being guilty of murder, theft, adultery, it may be possible to keep the law; but if we understand the full meaning of the law we shall find that it brings us a sense of guilt and a knowledge of our need for a Saviour.

Evidently the ruler felt that he had not received a complete answer. He said to Jesus, "What lack I yet?" And Jesus replied: "If thou wilt be perfect, go and sell that thou hast, and give to the poor, and thou shalt have treasure in heaven: and come and follow me." (Matthew 19:20-21.) We pass here from religion as obedience to a moral code to religion as commitment to a Person. At the heart of the Christian faith there is a Person who demands our complete allegiance.

Our difficulty with this word of Jesus to the young ruler is with the command: "Go and sell that thou hast, and give to the poor, and thou shalt have treasure in heaven." We cannot universalize this and say that a condition of following Jesus is the giving of all our possessions to the poor. Jesus did not make the vow of poverty a condition of being accepted as a disciple. Peter continued to have his home in Capernaum; and while the disciples were not rich in this world's goods, they were not beggars. Jesus indicates the real problem in the ruler's life when He says to His disciples: "Children, how hard is it for them that trust in riches to enter into the kingdom of God!" (Mark 10:24.) Jesus saw that the young man's trust in his riches stood in the way of his full surrender of life. He put His finger unerringly on the thing in the young man's life that made it difficult for him to enter the Kingdom of God. He asked him to be willing to give up his trust in his wealth and to be ready to come to Him as a disciple without reservation.

The demand which Jesus makes here stands in sharp perspective because of the vastness of the ruler's possessions, but it is not essentially different from the demand which He made on others. Peter and Andrew and the sons of Zebedee left their boats and nets and fishing business to follow Jesus. Matthew walked away from the seat of custom. Saul of Tarsus came to the point where he counted as refuse the things he had once considered most worthwhile in order that he might gain Christ and the hope of attaining unto the resurrection of the dead.

The rich young ruler stands on the threshold of the Kingdom of God. If he had been willing to give up his trust in his wealth he might have found an honored place among the followers of Jesus. He might have found the secret to the most abiding satisfactions of this life, and he might have found his life in this world a preparation for the eternal life which Jesus has promised to His followers. But he makes the great refusal and turns away. We cannot fail to contrast the eagerness and expectancy with which he comes running to Jesus and the slow, sorrowful steps with which he walks away. The cost of discipleship has been too great. He has heard the call to follow Jesus but he has turned back to his trust in his possessions.

"Then came to him the mother of Zebedee's children."—Matthew 20:20.

16. SALOME

Scripture background: Matthew 20:20-28; Mark 10:35-45; 15:40-41; 16:1; Acts 12:2.

There are two women named Salome whom we meet in the pages of the New Testament. The daughter of Herodias who danced before Herod the Tetrarch was called Salome. Her name is not actually given in Scripture. Matthew and Mark both refer to her merely as the daughter of Herodias. We learn from Josephus that she was named Salome.* She was an evil woman, the daughter of a wicked mother. She is known to all students of Scripture because she asked for and received the head of John the Baptist on a charger. Because of the notoriety which has been given to this request we are apt to think of Herodias' daughter when we hear the name Salome.

But among those who followed Jesus in the days of His flesh there was a noble woman who bore the name Salome. She is introduced to us in Matthew 20:20 as the mother of Zebedee's children. Matthew refers to her in the same manner in chapter 27, verse 56. We have to turn to Mark 15:40 and 16:1 to learn that her name was Salome. It is the fate of some people to be known because of their relation to someone who is very close to them. Probably Zebedee was an outstanding man in Galilee, and in the beginning Salome may have been identified as Zebedee's wife. Salome gave birth to two sons. Her first-born was named James, and the second son was called John. When these two boys grew to manhood she became known as the mother of Zebedee's children. As young men James and John were not "gentle-mannered, meek, and mild." Instead they were known as sons of thunder. We see their hot indignation, for example, in the story of their reaction when Jesus was not received by a village of the Samaritans. (Luke 9:51-56.)

Salome was known as the mother of Zebedee's children. Regardless of the way in which the name was given to her, it does represent that peculiar relation in which a man and woman are placed through the coming of their children. Through Salome, Zebedee knew the experience of being a husband and a father. As he thought of her he knew that he was bound to her by the simple fact that she was the mother of his children. This set her in a relation to him that was irrevocable.

We learn something of Salome when we think of her as the mother of James and John. We know that James and John stood

* Josephus, *Antiquities* xviii. 5, 4.

within the inner circle of the twelve disciples. On several occasions Jesus chose them along with Peter to be with Him in His times of decision and testing. We are certain to see something of the mother in the lives of the boys. There is a familiar proverb,

"Like mother, like son," is the saying so true,
The world will judge largely of "Mother" by you.*

We can be sure that the home which Zebedee and Salome made together was founded on their common faith in the God of Israel. It was a home which shared the Messianic expectation of the Jews of the time. James and John were disciples of John the Baptist before they became followers of Jesus. While following John in Judea, the sons of Zebedee first met Jesus of Nazareth. (John 1:40-42. Probably one of these two men was John.)

One day Zebedee and his boys went fishing. Fishing for them was not a sport, but a business. They had boats and nets and hired servants. While James and John were mending their nets in a boat beside the seashore, Jesus passed by and said to them, "Follow me." The sons of Zebedee left their father in the ship with the hired servants and followed Him. When Zebedee came home to Salome that night the boys were not with him. We do not know just how Salome reacted to the departure of her sons, but we do know that in time Salome also became a follower of Jesus. She was one of a comparatively small group of women who followed Him in some of His preaching tours of Galilee. (Mark 15:40-41.) These women also ministered unto Jesus of their substance. (Luke 8:3.) We can be sure that Zebedee and Salome did their part in supplying the common purse from which the disciples' expenses were paid. Salome was among the women who followed Jesus out of Galilee as He made His last visit to Jerusalem.

It was as Jesus was nearing Jerusalem that Salome came to Him with her two sons and asked that one of them might sit on His right hand and the other on His left when He came into His King-

* Margaret Johnston Grafflin, "To My Son."

dom. We must not miss the meaning of the symbolism. In the kingdoms of the ancient world, the man who was next in power to the king sat on his right hand and the one who was second in power sat on his left. Salome is asking Jesus to promise in advance to give her sons the two most important positions in the Kingdom which He is to establish.

Salome's request is in a sense an expression of her faith. As Jesus goes to Jerusalem He faces the united opposition of the leaders of Judaism, but Salome still believes that He will restore the Kingdom to Israel. We must have some sympathy with the mother's desire that her sons shall have positions of pre-eminence in the Kingdom of God. Jesus tells Salome that she does not understand the real nature of her request. She does not understand that greatness in the Kingdom of God is not something which can be promised as a candidate for president can promise his followers positions in his cabinet. Greatness in the Kingdom of God is something that has to be deserved. It is to be measured not in terms of power and authority but by the ability to serve.

Jesus reminds Salome and her sons that there is a spiritual price which must be paid for outstanding leadership in His service. He looks James and John in the eye and says: "Are ye able to drink of the cup that I shall drink of, and to be baptized with the baptism that I am baptized with?" We cannot be perfectly sure of His meaning here, but the baptism to which He refers is probably the completeness of His dedication to the will of God. In another setting He says: "I have a baptism to be baptized with; and how am I straitened till it be accomplished!" (Luke 12:50.) When Jesus speaks of the cup which He must drink, He is thinking of His readiness as the Suffering Servant to endure suffering and death. There is a sense in which Jesus' experience is unique. His followers cannot enter fully into the meaning of His baptism, and they cannot bear the full weight of His cross. But He is saying that no one can know greatness in the Kingdom of God without knowing something of His hatred of sin and something of His compassion for a lost world. He is saying, too, that those who follow Him must be ready to die for Him if necessary. All too often we pray to be made Christlike in character without understanding the meaning of our prayer. When we seek greatness in the Kingdom of God for those we love, are we ready for them to enter into the fellowship of the sufferings of Jesus and be conformed to His death? If Salome had understood the nature of her request, would she have brought her sons to Jesus?

Probably James and John understood better than their mother the searching question of Jesus. To His "Are ye able?" they reply "We are able." And Jesus answers: "Ye shall drink indeed of my cup, and be baptized with the baptism that I am baptized with."

At the time Salome did not fully understand the saying of Jesus. She knew the intensity of His sense of mission, but she was not prepared for His death. Events moved rapidly. In a few days Jesus was arrested, tried, and condemned. Salome joined a group of women who stood on the fringes of the crowd which gathered around the place of crucifixion. She was present when death came to Jesus of Nazareth. Perhaps at this time she thought of His words to her sons: "Ye shall indeed drink of my cup." Was this what she had asked for her sons?

The women remained at the cross. They were there during the earthquake and the supernatural darkness. They were present when Joseph of Arimathaea and Nicodemus came for the body of Jesus. They followed them to the tomb in Joseph's garden, and Salome was with the women who came on Sunday morning to the sepulcher. She saw the empty tomb and she heard the words of the angel: "He is not here: for he is risen, as he said." (Matthew 28:6.)

Salome had asked for pre-eminence for her sons. In time she knew what it was to give her first-born son as the first of the apostles to seal his faith with his life. About fourteen years after the death of Jesus, Herod the king "stretched forth his hands to vex certain of the church. And he killed James the brother of John with the sword." (Acts 12:1-2.) Salome knew a mother's sorrow, but she was comforted by the knowledge that James had lived nobly and died bravely. She knew, too, that death for her son meant that he went to be forever with his Lord. John, her second son, probably outlived all the other apostles. He was the apostle who understood best the heart and mind of his Lord. The sons of Salome did become great in the Kingdom of God.

> *"Jesus said unto her, I am the resurrection, and the life."—John 11:25.*

17. MARTHA

Scripture background: Luke 10:38-42; John 11:1-46; 12:2.

Luke writes: "Now it came to pass, as they went, that he [Jesus] entered into a certain village: and a certain woman named Martha received him into her house." (Luke 10:38.) The characters of Martha and Mary are set forth clearly in the story which follows. Martha is cumbered with much serving and she has a tendency to be dictatorial, but her failures here are the exaggeration of her virtues. She was practical and efficient, and she was concerned that Jesus as her guest should have the best. It would have been better if she had been less interested in the dinner and more ready to sit with Mary at the feet of Jesus to hear His word. However, we cannot fail to appreciate Martha as she bears the responsibility of the home. The references to Martha and Mary in the Fourth Gospel fall into the pattern which is set in Luke. When Jesus comes to the home after Lazarus' death, Mary is weeping and Martha is receiving the guests. Martha cannot refrain from reminding Jesus at the tomb of Lazarus that her brother has been dead four days and that there will be an odor.

When the dinner is given to Jesus and His disciples in the home of Simon the leper, Mary breaks the bottle of ointment and Martha serves the meal.

Jesus came frequently to Martha's home as a guest, but He was not near Bethany when sickness and death came to her home. We can be sure that Martha with her usual efficiency nursed her sick brother, but Lazarus did not improve. In time the sisters sent for

Jesus. They knew enough of the healing ministry of Jesus to be confident that He could save their brother, but Jesus did not come and Lazarus died. It was necessary, therefore, to bury the body. The sisters returned from the tomb to the empty home.

When Jesus and His disciples finally reached the edge of the little village of Bethany, Lazarus had been dead four days. Martha heard that Jesus was coming and went to meet Him, but Mary sat still in the house. As Martha meets Jesus she is a sorrowing woman in the midst of her dead. What will she say to Jesus? More important, what will He say to her?

Martha begins with the statement: "Lord, if you had been here, my brother would not have died. And even now I know that whatever you ask from God, God will give you." (John 11:21-22, R.S.V.) This is an expression of faith in Jesus. With it there is an expression of hope, a hope which is not defined but is based on her confidence in Jesus. He says to Martha: "Thy brother shall rise again." (John 11:23.) We cannot be certain of the meaning Jesus intended to convey. He may have been predicting the miracle which He was to perform, or He may have been affirming the Jewish hope of a resurrection. The Jews were divided on this point. The Pharisees held strongly to the hope of the resurrection of the dead, but the Sadducees denied it. Jesus did not crush this hope of the Pharisees. He affirmed it and attached it to Himself. He sets forth His teaching concerning the resurrection in John 5:25-29, and three times in the sixth chapter of John He says of the believer, "I will raise him up at the last day." (John 6:40, 44, 54.)

Jesus may have been referring to His bringing of Lazarus back from the dead, but Martha understands Him to refer to the hope of the resurrection at the last day. She affirms her faith in this as she says, "I know that he shall rise again in the resurrection at the last day." But this knowledge does not seem to bring much comfort to Martha's heart. She believes in the dim hope of a resurrection at the last day, but she wants to know whether or not her brother is alive now.

Jesus speaks to Martha's need as He utters the familiar words:

"I am the resurrection, and the life: he that believeth on me, though he die, yet shall he live; and whosoever liveth and believeth on me shall never die." (John 11:25-26, A.S.V.) When Jesus says, "I am the resurrection," He reaffirms the hope of the resurrection of the dead at the last day. What does He mean when He says, "I am . . . the life: he that believeth on me, though he die, yet shall he live"? He is telling Martha that for the person who believes on Him, death is not the end. He is saying that the one who believes on Him will survive the crisis of the separation of soul and body. He is giving her the assurance that her brother is united to Him and is alive. What does He mean when He adds in verse 26, "and whosoever liveth and believeth on me shall never die"? He cannot mean that those who believe on Him do not pass through the experience of physical death. Millions have believed on Him and have passed through death into the Great Beyond. We can spiritualize the verse and interpret it to mean that those who believe on Jesus do not die eternally. This makes it a repetition of the thought of verse 25. It is possible, however, to apply this verse to the life beyond the grave. Jesus may mean that those believers who have passed through the experience of death enter into a life in which there is no second death. There is an old legend that when Lazarus came back from the grave he said to Jesus, "Lord, must I die again?" According to the legend Jesus said to him, "Yes, you must die again."* But if Lazarus had met the Christ in the life that lies beyond the grave and asked the same question he would have received a different answer. Jesus could then have said: "No, Lazarus, you have passed through death into an endless life." This is pure legend but it illustrates the truth that the believers who have survived the crisis of physical death enter into a world in which they do not have to face again disintegration and death. Jesus tells Martha that those who believe on Him survive the separation of soul and body and enter into a world in which there is no more death.

Having made this claim, He says to Martha, "Believest thou

* *Cambridge Bible for Schools and Colleges, St. John,* edited by Alfred Plummer, p. 241. Published by the Cambridge University Press.

this?" And Martha replies: "Yea, Lord: I have believed that thou art the Christ, the Son of God, even he that cometh into the world." (John 11:26-27, a.s.v.) It may be at this point that Jesus speaks to Martha the words referred to in verse 40 when He says: "Said I not unto thee, that, if thou wouldest believe, thou shouldest see the glory of God?"

The claim which Jesus makes here is tremendous. He proclaims Himself as the resurrection and the life. He says that those who believe on Him will survive the crisis of death and live on in a world that is beyond death. He promises a life that is not marked by existence unto death. He identifies Himself with the hope for an ultimate resurrection at the last day. If these words are true they are sufficient to bring comfort and hope to the sorrowing heart of Martha. We should notice, too, that His words have no specific reference to Lazarus. They are spoken to Martha as she grieves for Lazarus, but they apply to all who believe on Jesus as Lord and Saviour. The words were first spoken to Martha, but they have since been spoken to countless millions of Christians who have stood in the presence of their dead.

Jesus Himself is aware of the stupendous nature of the claims which He makes for Himself as He comforts the sorrowing heart of Martha. As He stands at the tomb of Lazarus He lifts His eyes and says, "Father, I thank thee that thou hast heard me. I knew that thou hearest me always, but I have said this on account of the people standing by, that they may believe that thou didst send me." (John 11:41-42, r.s.v.) The miracle which follows is the sign to those who stand by, and through them to all men, that the Father has sent Jesus. It is the divine authentication of the tremendous claims that Jesus has made.

This was the sign to Martha. There has been given to us a greater sign. The final stamp of approval on the claims of Jesus of Nazareth was given to His followers when God brought Him again from the dead and gave through Him a manifestation on earth of the resurrection life. Paul tells the Romans that Jesus Christ was declared to be the Son of God with power by the resurrection from the dead. The Christian Church was the community of those who received the witness of the apostles to Jesus' resurrection.

Jesus comes to Martha as she grieves for Lazarus. He says to her: "I am the resurrection, and the life: he that believeth on me, though he die, yet shall he live; and whosoever liveth and believeth on me shall never die. *Believest thou this?*" Martha replies: "Yea, Lord: I have believed that thou art the Christ, the Son of God, even he that cometh into the world." (John 11:25-27, A.S.V.) Jesus also tells Martha that if she believes, she will see the glory of God. Martha saw that day the revelation of God's glory as her brother Lazarus was restored to life. She saw the full glory of God when she entered through death into the resurrection world of God through her faith in Jesus as her Lord and Saviour.

"This also that she hath done shall be spoken of for a memorial of her."—Mark 14:9.

18. MARY OF BETHANY

Scripture background: Matthew 26:6-13; Mark 14:3-9; Luke 10:38-42; John 11:1-46; 12:1-10.

Jesus must have loved to visit the home in Bethany. John says simply: "Now Jesus loved Martha, and her sister, and Lazarus." The probability is that Jesus stayed in this home during most of His visits to Jerusalem and that during the last week of His life it was the home from which He went forth to His encounter with the leaders of the Jews in Jerusalem. (Matthew 21:17; Mark 11:1,11.) Our first account of a visit of Jesus to this home is found in Luke 10:38-42. Luke tells us that during this visit Martha was "cumbered about much serving," but that Mary "sat at Jesus' feet, and heard his word." Martha does not stand out well in this story. She is critical of Mary. She comes to Jesus saying, "Lord, dost thou not care that my sister hath left me to serve alone? bid her therefore that she help me." Martha seems to feel that Jesus is lacking in His concern for her as she is left alone in the kitchen, and she ventures to suggest that He should tell Mary to help in the work of the home.

A case can be made for Martha's point of view. There is a certain amount of work that has to be done in every home. Mary as a member of the household was under obligation to do her share of the work that had to be done. But Jesus defends Mary. It is very easy to be so busy in serving a guest that we do not have time for fellowship with those we entertain. Mary had to choose between joining Martha in her concern for much serving or sitting at Jesus' feet and hearing His word. She chose the latter and Jesus commended her for her choice. Martha was concerned and troubled about many things and was missing the opportunity of hearing the things that Jesus had to say to her. It would have been better to have had more simplicity in serving and more time to listen to Jesus talk. Mary was laying hold of imperishable values at a time when Martha was absorbed in much serving. The message of this story comes home to all who read it. It is so easy for us to be so absorbed in the cares of this life that we fail to hear the word Jesus would speak to us if we would take time to listen.

The second scene in Mary's life comes in connection with the sickness and death of Lazarus. Mary and Martha must have ministered together to their sick brother, and Mary must have entered into the decision to send for Jesus in spite of the danger involved in His return to Judea. However, Mary was not with Martha when she met Jesus on the edge of the village, and she did not hear Jesus' words to Martha in which He declared that He was the resurrection and the life. Immediately after this conversation with Martha, Jesus must have asked for Mary. We know that Martha called Mary secretly, saying, "The Master is come, and calleth for thee." Mary arose immediately and went to Jesus, to greet Him with the words: "Lord, if thou hadst been here, my brother had not died." It was when Jesus saw Mary weeping that He, too, groaned in the spirit and was troubled and burst into tears. It was in this setting that Jesus called Lazarus back from the grave and restored him to his sisters. Mary added to her deep love for Jesus the gratitude of a woman who knew that because of Jesus her brother was alive.

The third scene in the life of Mary takes place in the home of Simon the leper. This story is told for us in Matthew 26:6-13, Mark 14:3-9, and John 12:1-9. It needs to be carefully distinguished from a somewhat similar story told in Luke 7:36-50. Jesus and His disciples were invited to a meal in the home of a man named Simon. He may have been a leper whom Jesus had healed. Lazarus was one of the guests. Martha served. During this meal Mary came into the dining room with a pound of very expensive ointment. She anointed the head and feet of Jesus and proceeded to wipe His feet with the hairs of her head. The aroma of the ointment filled the room. The evangelists are agreed that the ointment was of the most expensive variety. Judas and the disciples estimated its value at three hundred pence. A penny was about the wage of a common laborer for a day. The disciples were shocked at the extravagance and waste in using a valuable ointment in this way.

Again Jesus defends Mary. He knows that she has wanted in some way to express her love for Him and that she has done this as her way of revealing her love and gratitude. He suggests, too, that Mary has done this deed with a sense of urgency. We need not be surprised to learn that Mary expected Jesus' death at the hand of the Jewish authorities. She knew full well the strength of the opposition to Jesus, and Jesus had been consistently telling His disciples that He must go to Jerusalem to suffer and die. Mary was ready to sit at Jesus' feet and hear His word. Probably with her woman's intuition she understood better than the disciples the meaning of the way in which Jesus had identified Himself with the suffering servant of Isaiah. She knew that time was running out. She loved with a love that did not count the cost and she wanted a way to show her love and gratitude before it was too late.

When Jesus said, "The poor always ye have with you," He did not mean to say that poverty is inevitable; and no one could accuse Him of lack of compassion for the poor. The vision of the poor was always with Him, and He gave Himself without stint to a preaching and healing ministry to the poor of His generation. Jesus emphasized the brevity of the time that was left to Him before His passion, and Mary was right in feeling that she could not delay. We are true to her spirit when we say that the time to show our love to people is while they are with us.

Jesus' approval of Mary's gift indicates His blessing on some acts of spending which may seem extravagant. We must not forget the poor, and we must be prepared to live simply in order that we may give largely; but a proper concern for the poor should not prevent some spending for others in which we reveal a love which is not always counting the cost. There is a place, for example, for sacrificial giving to provide beauty and dignity in the place of worship.

Jesus says of Mary: "Wheresoever this gospel shall be preached throughout the whole world, this also that she hath done shall be spoken of for a memorial of her." These are remarkable words. They are spoken immediately after He has said of her, "She is come aforehand to anoint my body to the burying." Jesus knows, and He feels that Mary knows, that His death is near. This anointing can be thought of as a preparation of His body for the tomb. He is confident, however, that the gospel which centers in the proclamation of the meaning of His death will be preached to the whole world, and He knows that Mary's deed will stand forever as a memorial to her. John has selected Mary as one of those who knew Jesus and responded to Him in love and gratitude. Her act of anointing His body has been done with no thought of herself. Her one concern has been to reveal in some way before it is too late a love which she knows she cannot adequately express. It may have been foolish for her to spend her all on a bottle of ointment whose fragrance was soon lost forever. It might have been better to use the money in a ministry to the poor, but the deed of Mary pointed to a heart that was filled with love. Jesus saw beyond the deed to the love which it expressed. His words are fulfilled today, because we cannot think of Mary of Bethany apart from our consciousness of the depth and wonder of her love for her Lord.

Jesus saw in this act the revelation of a love which did not count the cost. He knew that in the same act the shadow of His coming death fell upon the banquet scene. He knew, too, that in a much deeper sense His death was an expression of God's love which did not count the cost. God had not spared His own Son. Jesus had loved His own—He loved them enough to die for them. He knew that there was no greater love than that in which a man laid down His life for His friends. Mary's deed was not necessary. She did not have to buy this bottle of ointment to anoint the body of her Lord. In contrast, the death of Christ did have to take place. His death was rooted in the necessity of an atonement. He knew that He could not at the same time save others and save Himself. He had to drink the cup which His Father presented to Him if He was to be the Saviour of mankind. Just because His death was a ransom for many that had to be paid, it reveals more profoundly than Mary's deed the love which did not count the cost.

"This sickness is . . . for the glory of God."—John 11:4.

19. LAZARUS

Scripture background: John 11:1—12:19.

The raising of Lazarus is the culmination of the signs in the development of John's Gospel. The beginning of signs was the turning of water into wine. The movement of the Gospel from the Prologue to the beginning of Passion Week is built around a series of selected incidents in Jesus' life. John has chosen them as situations in which Jesus manifests His glory and calls forth faith from His followers. They fulfill the word to Nathanael: "Thou shalt see greater things than these." (John 1:50.) These signs include the turning of water into wine, the healing of the nobleman's son, the healing of the impotent man at the pool of

Bethesda, the multiplication of the loaves and fishes, the walking on the sea, and the healing of the man born blind. They are all miraculous signs in which a supernatural power is at work. We cannot say that one is more difficult than the other. None of them is possible apart from the power of God, and if Jesus was the medium of the power of the eternal God, such signs are appropriate to Him. If we accept Jesus' resurrection from the dead as the central event of the Christian faith, we must admit that the other signs are possible.

The raising of Lazarus is a sign which concerns us all. It is in connection with this sign that Jesus makes the great statement: "I am the resurrection, and the life: he that believeth on me, though he die, yet shall he live; and whosoever liveth and believeth on me shall never die." (John 11:25-26, a.s.v.) These words are spoken at practically every Christian funeral. They are a great statement of the Christian hope that those who die in the Lord survive the crisis of separation of soul and body and remain united to Christ in a world that lies beyond the grave. The sign is given in confirmation of this great statement. The great spiritual truths which the writer of the Fourth Gospel sets forth are his interpretation of the significance of the signs which Jesus had given.

When Lazarus is sick the sisters send to Jesus saying, "Lord, behold, he whom thou lovest is sick." (John 11:3.) John gives the setting as he writes: "Now Jesus *loved* Martha, and her sister, and Lazarus." (John 11:5.) In commenting on this statement Plummer says: "The English Version loses much here, and still more in 21:15-17, by using the same word 'love' to translate two different Greek words: nor can the loss be remedied satisfactorily. The word used in verse 3, *philein*, denotes a passionate, emotional warmth, which loves and cares not to ask why; the affection of lovers, parents, and the like. The word used here, *agapân*, denotes a calm, discriminating attachment, which loves because of the excellence of the loved object; the affection of friends. *Philein* is the stronger, but less reasoning; *agapân* the more earnest, but less intense. The sisters naturally use the more emotional word, describing their own feeling towards their brother; the evangelist equally naturally uses the loftier and less impulsive word. The fact that the sisters are here included is not the reason for the change of expression."* Jesus loved all men. He prayed for His enemies. But this did not prevent Him from discriminating between people and loving some people for what they were. In a similar way He had a unique love for John in the band of disciples. We learn much about Lazarus from the simple fact that Jesus loved him with that discriminating love which is based on the excellence of the object loved.

Sickness came to Lazarus. Jesus describes this sickness as "not unto death, but for the glory of God." (John 11:4.) He was thinking of the revelation of His compassion and His power which was to be given in the raising of Lazarus. But for Lazarus this was sickness unto death. It soon became evident both to the sisters and to Lazarus himself that he had been seized with an illness which promised to be fatal. It was then that the sisters sent for Jesus. They knew enough of His healing ministry to believe that He could check the progress of the disease and save their brother's life. But Jesus did not come. Instead death came to Lazarus.

It is idle for us to speculate on where the spirit of Lazarus was during those four days that his body was in the tomb. All that we have to go on in this story is the word of Jesus to Martha: "I am the resurrection, and the life: he that believeth on me, though he die, yet shall he live." (John 11:25, A.S.V.) Robert Browning in his "Epistle of Karshish" pictures Lazarus some thirty years later as he is living in Bethany. He describes him as one who is in this world but not of it, as one whose sense of values seems to be determined by reference to a world he cannot describe. The probability is that a veil was drawn over any experiences that may have been his during that four days. With the skill of a great artist Browning describes the struggle between faith and

---

* *Cambridge Bible for Schools and Colleges, St. John,* edited by Alfred Plummer, p. 229. (Slightly adapted.) Published by the Cambridge University Press. By permission.

doubt in the soul of Karshish as he faces the story of Lazarus and
Lazarus' witness to Jesus as God manifest in the flesh. He writes:

"This man so cured regards the curer, then,
As—God forgive me! who but God Himself,
Creator and sustainer of the world,
That came and dwelt in flesh on it awhile!
—'Sayeth that such an one was born and lived,
Taught, healed the sick, broke bread at his own house,
Then died, with Lazarus by, for aught I know,
And yet was . . ."*

And in the closing verses of this poem Karshish realizes the
significance of the story of Lazarus:

"The very God! think, Abib; dost thou think?
So, the All-Great, were the All-Loving too—
So, through the thunder comes a human voice
Saying, 'O heart I made, a heart beats here!
Face, my hands fashioned, see it in myself!
Thou hast no power nor mayst conceive of mine,
But love I gave thee, with myself to love,
And thou must love me who have died for thee!'
The madman saith He said so: it is strange."†

The sign of the raising of Lazarus, like the other signs recorded in John, was a manifestation of the glory of God and a
call to faith. Many of the Jews who came to comfort Mary and
saw what Jesus did believed on Him. But the Gospel of John
traces both the development of faith and the hardening of unbelief. The enemies of Jesus were forced to deal with the last
and greatest of the signs. They admitted that Jesus had performed many miracles. They had no explanation to give for these
miracles, but they were not prepared to accept their implications.
So the process of hardening moved into its final stage in which
the Pharisees and the chief priests united to destroy Jesus.

* Robert Browning, "Epistle of Karshish."
† Ibid.

Through that strange blindness which comes as we harden our hearts, Lazarus' life was again in danger. By his very existence he was a witness to Jesus' power. As far as we know, these evil designs concerning Lazarus were not executed. The last picture we have of him in the New Testament is when he sits as the guest of Simon the leper as his sister Mary pours the oil of spikenard on the head and feet of Jesus.

There is a profound difference between the raising of Lazarus and the resurrection of Jesus. Strictly speaking, the raising of Lazarus is a resuscitation. Life returns to the body which has been dead for four days, but the pattern of life is not altered. Lazarus still lives a life marked by existence which moves toward death. It is appointed unto man once to die, but Lazarus had the unique experience of dying twice.

Jesus, however, passed through death to the resurrection world of God. That which called the New Testament Church into being was not the empty tomb; it was the vision of the risen Lord in the glory of His resurrection body. With their earth-bound eyes, the disciples could not see the fullness of this glory, but they did come into contact with a glorified Person who by His very existence bore witness to the reality of the resurrection world which lies beyond this visible world of time and space.

Jesus' resurrection from the dead, like the raising of Lazarus, is a sign. It is the final sign which God has given that men might believe that Jesus is the Christ, the Son of God; and that believing they might have life in His name. Through the witness of the disciples to the risen Lord the New Testament Church was called into being.

In connection with the raising of Lazarus, Jesus puts forth the tremendous claim: "I am the resurrection, and the life: he that believeth on me, though he die, yet shall he live." (John 11:25, A.S.V.) The miracle of the raising of Lazarus was a sign to Martha and those who were with her of Jesus' power to keep His promise: "he that believeth," etc. It gave them the assurance that the Father had sent Jesus. For those of us who look back upon Jesus' finished work, this sign does not stand alone. We have also the apostles' witness to the risen Lord. Our confidence that Jesus is able to keep us in the hour of death is rooted in our belief in His resurrection. Peter speaks for the Christian community when he writes: "Blessed be the God and Father of our Lord Jesus Christ! By his great mercy we have been born anew to a living hope through the resurrection of Jesus Christ from the dead, and to an inheritance which is imperishable, undefiled, and unfading, kept in heaven for you." (1 Peter 1:3-5, R.S.V.)

Faces of the Twelve

"And the Lord turned, and looked upon Peter."—
Luke 22:61.

20. SIMON PETER

*Scripture background: Matthew 16:13-23; 26:33-35,
51-53, 69-75; Mark 14:27-31, 65-72; Luke 22:31-34,
54-62; John 6:66-71; 18:10-11, 15-18.*

Peter, the leader and spokesman of the twelve disciples, denied his Lord. The story of his fall is a warning to all who
are overconfident in the time of temptation, but the fact of his
restoration to leadership gives encouragement to all who fall and
seek to rise again. We see in the story of Peter the full dimensions
of the struggle between good and evil which goes on in the human soul. Satan wanted Peter that he might sift him as wheat, but
Jesus prayed for him that his faith might not fail.

We need not be surprised that Satan wanted Peter. Satan had
the audacity to seek to tempt the Christ, and he did not depart
from Jesus until he had exhausted every temptation. Men do not
cease from temptation when they move into exalted positions.
The nature and character of their temptations may change, but
those who stand in positions of opportunity and power know a
range of temptation which is not fully realized by those of lesser
stature. It would have been a great victory for evil if Peter could
have been permanently turned aside from following the Christ.

Satan wanted Peter that he might sift him as wheat. Satan
seeks to test the genuineness of Peter's faith and to undermine his
loyalty to Jesus. We have here in an incidental way some understanding of the place of Satan as he is permitted by God to con-

tinue in a moral universe. Faith must be tested if genuine faith is to stand out as distinct from the spurious variety. Our loyalty to Jesus must be strong enough to control our life even when it looks as if following Him will lead to prison and death.

Satan intends to use the experience of Calvary to test the faith of Peter. Peter had come to faith in Jesus as the Christ. At Caesarea Philippi he boldly declared that Jesus was the Christ, the Son of the living God. Jesus accepted his declaration of faith and told him that this was an insight born of the work of the Spirit of God in his heart. But when Jesus went on to explain to Peter that as the Christ He must suffer and die, Peter rejected at once this identification of the Messiah with the Suffering Servant and insisted that such thoughts should be far from his Lord. Jesus in turn pronounced the suggestion of Peter as Satanic. Now the hour of crisis draws near when Jesus must go to prison and death. It is in this experience that Satan seeks to break Peter's faith in Jesus as the Christ.

Jesus' prayer that the faith of Peter may not fail reveals the true citadel of the soul in the struggle with evil. Peter will not fail in action unless he begins to doubt the validity of his convictions concerning Jesus. There is a sense in which the soul is tempted only by the good or by that which at the time seems to the person to be good for him. If we lie, it is because we feel that for us at that time the lie is better than the truth. If we as Christians deny our Lord it is because we are not sure that the way to which He points is best for us. The failure to follow Him grows out of an uncertainty about whether in all cases He must be acknowledged as Lord. The citadel of the soul in the struggle with evil is an unquestioning faith in the Lordship of Jesus and in the goodness of His purpose for us.

Jesus knows that the events connected with His arrest, His trial, and His death will be a time of testing for His disciples. He prepares them for the experience they are to face by telling them that on that night they will all be offended in Him. He says that when the shepherd is smitten the sheep will be scattered abroad. Peter responds to the warning of Jesus by insisting that he will never deny his Lord. He says that he will be faithful even if all the other disciples deny Jesus. He professes his willingness to go with Jesus to prison and death. Peter meant what he said. He intended to be faithful to his Lord even unto death. But Jesus immediately warns him that a time of testing is coming and tells him that before the cock crows for morning he will have three times denied his Lord.

We do not need to trace in detail the familiar events of the night before the crucifixion. Peter goes to the Garden of Gethsemane with Jesus. Here he fails to stay awake while Jesus is praying and receives along with James and John the warning: "Watch and pray, that ye enter not into temptation: the spirit indeed is willing, but the flesh is weak." (Matthew 26:41.) This was part of the trouble with Peter. His resolutions went beyond his ability to perform. His spirit was willing but the flesh was weak. The experience of Peter at the time of the arrest probably had a profound effect upon him. Peter drew his sword and prepared to give battle to those who came to lay hold of his Lord. He struck a vicious blow at a servant of the high priest named Malchus, but Jesus commanded Peter to put up his sword and said that all who took the sword would perish with the sword. He would not permit His disciples to offer any violent resistance to those who came to arrest Him. Perhaps it was at this point that Peter began to wonder if he was mistaken in his acknowledgment of Jesus as the Messiah.

At the time of the arrest all the disciples but Peter and John deserted Jesus and fled. Because John was known to the high priest, he was able to enter the palace with Jesus. He also made it possible for Peter, who had followed at a distance, to enter the court. The story of Peter's denial is well known. He wants to be near Jesus and he seeks to hide his identity by losing himself in the crowd. But individuals in the crowd recognize him as a Galilean and as a follower of Jesus. Peter denies their charges and hopes still to remain unnoticed. One denial leads to another until he finds himself cursing and swearing as he insists that he has never heard of Jesus. It is obvious that Peter here is moved by the desire to remain unnoticed and by some concern for his own personal safety. But these considerations do not explain his conduct. They are symptoms of a deeper uncertainty in which Peter's whole life is involved. He has committed himself to Jesus as the Christ. He has left all and followed Him. He has been certain that Jesus would reveal Himself as the Deliverer of His people. But instead Jesus without a struggle has permitted Himself to be arrested. Peter knows that this is the prelude to the fulfillment of Jesus' prediction concerning His suffering and death. The whole experience has crushed the spirit of Peter. He no longer has the shield of faith with which to resist the fiery darts of the evil one.

There are two events which break the power of evil over Peter. One of these is the crowing of the cock. This recalls to him the words of Jesus. It helps to restore his confidence in Jesus as he sees fulfillment of the prediction of a few hours before. More important than the crowing of the cock is the appearance of Jesus. This probably happens as He is being taken from the examination before Annas to the trial before Caiaphas. As Peter is insisting that he does not know Jesus, Jesus is led through the court bound as a prisoner. And Jesus turns and looks upon Peter. Great artists have attempted to paint this scene. There must have been rebuke and sorrow in the look of Jesus. He never condoned sin. But His disapointment must have been mingled with compassion. The story of Peter's temptation underlies the first stanza of a hymn which reads:

> "In the hour of trial,
> Jesus, plead for me;
> Lest by base denial
> I depart from Thee:
> When Thou seest me waver,
> With a look recall,
> Nor for fear or favor
> Suffer me to fall."

The crowing of the cock and the look of Jesus arrest the attention of Peter and recall him to the faith he has denied. He goes out and weeps bitterly. He does not yet understand the meaning of Calvary, but he knows that he must continue to trust Jesus as his Lord.

We know that on the day of the resurrection the risen Lord made Himself known to Peter. John has preserved for us the beautiful story of the scene on the shores of Galilee in which Peter is fully restored and given his commission to serve his Lord. Jesus told Peter that when he was converted he was to strengthen his brethren. (Luke 22:32.) We can be sure that Peter told many times the story of his fall, that he might point to the infinite grace of his Lord. We must never seek to do evil that good may come. But those who have failed and, through repentance, have found forgiveness and restoration can witness to others of the grace of God and can pray that in the future their own faith will not fail.

"Come ye after me, and I will make you to become fishers of men."—Mark 1:17.

21. ANDREW

Scripture background: Matthew 4:18-22; Mark 1:16-20; Luke 5:1-11; John 1:35-42; 6:8; 12:22; Acts 1:13.

Andrew's first contact with Jesus of Nazareth was in Judea beyond Jordan where John was baptizing. The story of his meeting with Jesus is told in John 1:35-42. We learn from this story that Andrew was a disciple of John the Baptist before he became a disciple of Jesus. Probably Peter, Andrew, James, and John were ardent followers of John the Baptist. The expectation of the coming of the Christ in the near future was at the center of John's preaching. It was this that gave a note of urgency to his call to repentance. In the main, those who followed John the Baptist recognized Jesus as the Christ and those who rejected John's baptism failed also to understand the authority of Jesus.

In John 1:25-34 we have the witness of John the Baptist to Jesus. We do not know whether or not Andrew heard this testimony. We do know that the next day Andrew and another disciple, who is almost certainly John the son of Zebedee, were standing with John the Baptist.* At this time the Baptist pointed to Jesus as He walked by and said: "Behold the Lamb of God!" Immediately the two disciples left John the Baptist and followed Jesus. When Jesus saw them following Him, He said to them: "What seek ye?" They said to him: "Rabbi, where dwellest thou?" Jesus said to them: "Come and see." Andrew and his friend accepted the invitation of Jesus to go with Him to where He was staying. They remained with Jesus for the rest of that day.

We have no record of the conversation that went on as Jesus talked with these men. We do know that Andrew came out of this conversation with the profound conviction that Jesus was the Christ. He went at once to his brother Simon and said to him: "We have found the Messiah." (John 1:41, R.S.V.) Andrew brought his brother to Jesus. The suggestion of the story is that when Andrew went for Peter, John went for James. Andrew got back with Peter before John returned with James. It was at this time that Jesus said to Simon: "Thou art Simon the son of Jona: thou shalt be called Cephas, which is by interpretation, A stone." The words are prophetic. They suggest the way in which the son of Jonas will develop under the leadership of Jesus until he becomes indeed a rock, the bold and courageous leader of the band of disciples through whom Jesus was to establish His Church. When we think of Jesus' first meeting with Simon Peter, we are bound to remember the tremendous part that Peter plays in the narrative of the New Testament; but as we let our imagination play on the future of Peter we should not forget that Peter was brought to Jesus by his brother Andrew. Probably Andrew did not have a difficult time persuading Peter to come to Jesus. Both of the brothers were disciples of John who were looking for the

---

* For a brief discussion of this, see Alfred Plummer, *Cambridge Bible for Schools and Colleges, St. John*, p. 77.

coming of the Christ. But Andrew did have the satisfaction of having given his witness concerning the Christ and the joy of bringing his brother to Jesus.

There is no essential conflict between the story which John tells and the account of Jesus' meeting with these four disciples as we have it in the first three Gospels. When we know that they had been with Jesus in Judea, we can understand the readiness with which they left their nets and followed Him when He called them by the Sea of Galilee. Luke adds to the story of Matthew and Mark the account of the remarkable catch of fishes which followed Jesus' teaching from the boat and His words to Peter as the disciples sense the presence of the supernatural. "Fear not; from henceforth thou shalt catch men." (Luke 5:10.)

Andrew was the disciple who found and brought to Jesus the lad with the five barley loaves and two small fishes at the time of the feeding of the five thousand. Andrew looked at the loaves and the fishes and said to Jesus: "But what are they among so many?" (John 6:9.) His faith was weak, but at least he found a boy who had some food and brought him to Jesus. When the Greeks come asking to see Jesus they find Philip. Philip finds Andrew, and Andrew and Philip come and tell Jesus. (John 12:22.) In each of the three incidents in which he is mentioned specifically in the New Testament, Andrew is busy bringing people to Jesus.

Jesus did not see fit to include Andrew in the inner circle of His band of disciples. When He went to the home of Jairus and raised his daughter from the dead, He took with Him Peter and James and John. He did not take Andrew. When He went to the mountain of Transfiguration where His disciples were given a vision of His glory, He again took Peter and James and John. He left Andrew with the disciples who stayed in the valley. And at the time of the agony of prayer in Gethsemane, Andrew was not with the three who were nearest to Jesus. These incidents must have been typical of many others. We cannot enter into the decision of Jesus not to take Andrew with Him on these occasions, but we can be sure that His decision was wise and just. Andrew did not have the capacities for leadership that his brother Simon had. He was not a spiritual genius like John. And evidently James had possibilities which went beyond the gifts of Andrew. We can violate a man's personality by asking him to become the kind of person who is not the true development of his own self. There is no indication that Andrew resented in any way Jesus' decision concerning him. Whenever we see Andrew he is doing the thing he knows how to do. He is bringing men to Jesus.

It is appropriate therefore that we consider in our study of Andrew the word spoken to Simon and Andrew by the Sea of Galilee early in the ministry of Jesus. Jesus said to them: "Come ye after me, and I will make you to become fishers of men." (Mark 1:17.) The condition which is involved in this promise is expressed in the words, "Come ye after me." For Andrew, this involved at first the leaving of his fishing business to follow Jesus in His journeys through Galilee. But it soon became clear that the invitation, "Come ye after me," involved much more than walking with Jesus on His preaching missions. It involved accepting Jesus as Lord and Master. This meant the acknowledgment of Jesus' authority over his life and the effort to live in a way that was pleasing to Jesus. As Andrew increasingly understood the implications of Jesus' message he saw more fully the radical nature of the demands which Jesus made upon him. He learned in time that loyalty to Jesus meant the readiness to break with many of the established customs of his time. Following Jesus meant entering into the meaning of His offense and sharing the opposition of the world to all that Jesus stood for. Before Andrew could bring Peter to Jesus he had to reach for himself the conviction that Jesus was the Messiah. We cannot hope to lead others to Jesus until we have first surrendered ourselves to Him, and we cannot lead others any farther in the Christian life than we are willing to walk ourselves.

The call of Jesus to Andrew illustrates the nature of His call to men. He calls Andrew that through Andrew He may call others. He seeks to enable Andrew and Simon to become fishers of men. God calls men to be the instruments of His purpose. He calls

Abraham to found a holy family, that through him all the nations of the earth may be blessed. He calls Jeremiah to be a prophet to the nations. He calls Saul of Tarsus to become the Apostle to the Gentiles. Jesus chose the twelve disciples that they might be with Him and that He might send them forth to preach. He trained these men that they might be witnesses to Him to the ends of the earth.

The words of Jesus to Andrew should be meaningful to every local congregation. The Greek word translated "church" means the "called out." Jesus calls men to become His followers. He promises them the deepest satisfactions of this life and in the end, everlasting life. But the doctrine of the call should never be separated from the purpose of the call. If Jesus has called a group of people in a local community to be a believing community, He has called them that they may follow Him and that He may enable them to become fishers of men. He has called them to assume the responsibility for passing on the Christian heritage to the children of the Church. The faith of the parents must become alive in the hearts of the children. He has called each local congregation to assume its share of the world-wide responsibility of the Christian Church. A believing community which turns in on itself and ceases to face seriously the command to make disciples of all the nations will lose an essential note of New Testament Christianity. The Church must face its educational task and its missionary obligation. These responsibilities must never be separated from evangelism. But the supreme task of each believing community is for its members to follow Jesus until He fulfills His promise to enable them to become fishers of men. Andrew did not have the native ability of Peter or James or John. Jesus knew Andrew's limitations, and Andrew accepted his Lord's estimate of him. But there was one thing that Andrew could do. He could bring men to Jesus in the hope that they would find in Jesus their Saviour and Lord. He could lead men to Jesus in the confidence that Jesus would use them in the building of His Kingdom.

"Ye know not what manner of spirit ye are of."—Luke 9:55.

22. JAMES

Scripture background: Matthew 4:21; 10:2; 17:1; Mark 1:19-20, 29; 3:17; 5:37; 9:2; 10:35, 41; 13:3; 14:33; Luke 5:10; 6:14; 8:51; 9:28, 49-56; John 1:41; 21:2; Acts 1:13; 12:2.

James was the son of Zebedee and Salome and the brother of John. As he is always mentioned first, James was probably the older of the brothers. In all the references to him in Scripture, James is never mentioned apart from John with the one exception of the statement concerning his death in Acts 12:2. On the other hand, John is mentioned a number of times when there is no reference to James. John was probably the more gifted of the brothers, but James must have been a man of great possibilities, for Jesus included him along with Peter and John in the inner circle of the band of disciples. In their early manhood James and John were probably inseparable. In David's lament over Saul and Jonathan he says: "Saul and Jonathan were lovely and pleasant in their lives, and in their death they were not divided." (2 Samuel 1:23.) It could have been said of James and John that they were lovely and pleasant in their lives, but it could not have been said that in their death they were not divided. James was the first of the apostles to suffer martyrdom. He was executed by Herod Agrippa I about A.D. 44 under the royal policy of persecuting the Church to please the Jews. John probably outlived all the other apostles. He lived so long that the tradition arose that Jesus had said he could not die. In the last chapter of his Gospel, John corrects this tradition and insists that all Jesus had said to Peter was: "If I will that he tarry till I come, what is that to thee?" (John 21:23.)

While we know nothing about James apart from John, we

know enough of the things they did together to be sure that James, along with Peter and John, had an intimate knowledge of the life of Jesus of Nazareth. He probably was a disciple of John the Baptist, and his first contact with Jesus may have been in Judea. John was probably the disciple who, with Andrew, followed Jesus after John the Baptist testified to Him as the Lamb of God. We are safe in guessing that when Andrew went for Peter, John went for James, but we have no account of this first meeting of James with Jesus. A little later James and John were mending their nets by the Sea of Galilee when Jesus said to them: "Follow me." They left their nets and their father Zebedee in the boat with the hired servants and followed Jesus. (Matthew 4:21-22; Mark 1:19-20.) Along with Peter and John, James was overcome by the sense of the supernatural power of Jesus when he saw the great draught of fishes taken in obedience to Jesus' command. (Luke 5:10.) He was with Jesus when Peter's wife's mother was healed of her fever. (Mark 1:29.) Jesus took James with Him when He restored to life the daughter of Jairus. (Mark 5:37.) Peter and James and John were with Jesus on the Mount of Transfiguration. It was here that they saw the vision of the glory of their Lord. A little later James and John come to Jesus asking to sit at His right hand and His left when He comes into His Kingdom. (Mark 10:35-37.) James was one of four disciples to whom Jesus gave the discourse concerning the destruction of Jerusalem and the end of the world, found in Mark 13. Jesus took Peter and James and John to watch with Him in the hour of His agony of prayer in the Garden of Gethsemane. (Mark 14:33.) James was with the disciples when the risen Lord revealed Himself unto them. He was with the seven disciples to whom Jesus revealed Himself on the shores of the Sea of Galilee. (John 21:2.) The persecutor of the Church always loves to strike at an acknowledged leader. In his own way Herod paid a tribute to James when he selected him as the first of the apostles to be put to death.

Any one of the incidents to which we have referred would be worthy of careful study, but it may be more profitable in our understanding of James to concentrate on one incident we have not mentioned. Jesus taught James and John a needed lesson when in their hot indignation they wanted to call down fire from heaven to destroy a village of the Samaritans. (Luke 9:51-56.) James and John were known among their companions as sons of thunder; they were capable of fierce wrath. A man needs to have the capacity to get mad, but he needs also to learn to control his wrath. When they were angry these sons of Zebedee were like the flashing of lightning and the crashing of thunder. This was such an occasion.

Jesus had steadfastly set His face to go to Jerusalem. He was going because He knew that the time had come for Him to accomplish there His redemptive work. He was going to Jerusalem to die for the sins of the world. On His way it suited Him to spend a night in a village of the Samaritans. He sent messengers ahead to prepare the way for Him. But the Samaritans refused to receive Him because His face was as though He would go to Jerusalem.

When James and John heard of the refusal of the Samaritan village to receive Jesus, they were filled with indignation. Let it be said that their indignation was not because of an insult to them but because of the treatment accorded to their Lord. Their concern was for the honor and glory of Jesus. But in their wrath they suggested a terrible thing. They asked Jesus if He would be willing for them to call down fire from heaven to destroy the village of the Samaritans. They probably did not expect this to happen, but they had seen enough of the mighty works of their Lord to put no limits on His power.

The disciples' request called forth the rebuke of Jesus. His answer as it is given in the King James Version is not found in the best manuscripts. It may or may not be genuine. Plummer thinks that it is.* But it is certain that Jesus rebuked His disciples in some way, and the words attributed to Him here are in harmony with what He says of Himself in other places. (John 3:17.)

---

* See Plummer, *International Critical Commentary on Luke*, and the *Cambridge Bible on Luke*, p. 196, for discussions on both sides of this question.

James and John do not fully realize the implications of what they are saying, and they have failed to understand that the Son of man came not to destroy men's lives but to save them.

We need to heed the lesson of this story in a day when it is possible to drop bombs on cities and destroy the inhabitants. Jesus would teach His disciples not to destroy but to save. We are utterly foreign to His spirit when we think that we should seek to destroy those who have aroused our righteous indignation. We must aim even in anger to help those who resent us to attain the plan of God for them. The Samaritans had acted in a way that was inexcusable. They had refused to receive the One who was going to Jerusalem to die for their sins. The Jews never felt very kindly about the Samaritans, and even the disciples of Jesus were quick to resent an affront if it came from a Samaritan. But Jesus taught James the lesson of tolerance and patience in a situation filled with prejudice and tension.

This lesson needs to be continually learned afresh by the followers of Jesus. All too often Christians have persecuted each other in the name of their Lord. The same lesson needs to be learned in international situations. Nations act at times in ways which are expressions of fear, resentment, or the lust for power. On some occasions force may be necessary in international relations, but here also we must seek not to destroy but to save. The same spirit should mark us in the clash of race with race; we must not let any provocation cause us to give place to wrath. We must seek not to destroy but to help and save.

Perhaps this word of Jesus to James and John is most fitly spoken in the little tensions and feuds which mark our everyday life. It is easy to let our wrath flame forth on others and to wish that something would happen to them to get them out of our way, but the word of our Lord is to seek to help, not to destroy. James and John were sons of thunder. They were men of fierce temper and intense wrath. They needed to learn patience from Him "who, when he was reviled, reviled not again . . . but committed himself to him that judgeth righteously." (1 Peter 2:23.) They learned it as the weary disciples followed their Lord to another village.

"And he saw, and believed."—John 20:8.

23. JOHN

Scripture background: Matthew 20:20-28; Mark 10:35-45; John 13:23; 19:26; 20:1-10; 21: 7, 20.

In the Fourth Gospel, John is called the disciple whom Jesus loved. (John 19:26; 20:2; 21:20.) At the Lord's Supper he sat by Jesus and leaned his head on the Master's breast. There must have been a peculiar intimacy between Jesus and John. Probably John was closer to Jesus than any of the other disciples. When we say that John was the disciple whom Jesus loved we are led at once to ask whether or not Jesus showed partiality to John. We know that Jesus was a man of great compassion whose love went out to every human being. He looked upon the multitudes and was moved with compassion because they were as sheep without a shepherd. His love went out to those who sought to harm Him. On the cross He prayed for those who were crucifying Him. And in His lament over Jerusalem, the pathos of His wrath is that it is rooted in His love for Jerusalem. He loved His disciples and laid down His life for them.

But in love at its best there must be an element of discrimination. We love people for what they are and for what we believe they may become. Every great leader of men is inevitably forced to gather around him a small group of men who share his mind and heart. Jesus was no exception. From those who followed Him, He chose twelve men that they might be with Him and that He might send them forth to preach. Within the band of disciples there was an inner band of three. And within the inner circle of three, John stood out as the disciple who was closest to Jesus.

What was there about John that called forth in a peculiar way the love of Jesus? John was a man of temper. The sons of Zebedee were called sons of thunder. They were men of wrath. They had the capacity to get angry. On one occasion, John came into contact with a man who was casting out devils in the name of Jesus. John forbade him to use the name of Jesus when he was not identified with Jesus' disciples. But Jesus told John that he should not have done this, as those who were not against Him were for Him. (Luke 9:49-50.) John was with James when these sons of Zebedee felt that the Samaritans had insulted their Lord. In his wrath at the treatment Jesus had received, John was ready to pray for fire from heaven to destroy the village. Here also Jesus found it necessary to rebuke His disciple. We do not ask that a man be without temper. The man who has no capacity for anger is not apt to accomplish much in the world. We do ask that temper be brought under control. There is a proverb which says that "he that ruleth his spirit is better than he that taketh a city." (Proverbs 16:32.) Jesus wants men of temper, but He seeks to master them until their tempers are controlled and used in His service.

John was a man of ambition. He joined with James in the request for the highest places in the Kingdom which Jesus was to establish. Jesus must have selected the sons of Zebedee as His disciples in the full knowledge that they were men of intense ambition. A man who has no ambition and no drive is not apt to be much of a force either within or without the Kingdom of God. But Jesus had to teach John the difference between greatness in the secular world and greatness in the Kingdom of God. In the world, the great man is the man who can force others to serve him. In the Kingdom which Jesus established, greatness is measured in terms of capacity to serve. Jesus came not to be ministered unto but to minister. Greatness in the Kingdom of God involves inevitably the capacity to enter into Jesus' compassion for a lost world, the willingness to drink the cup which He drank and to be baptized with the baptism with which He was baptized. A tremendous spiritual price must be paid for greatness in the Kingdom of God.

Jesus loved John, and John responded to His love with a devotion which knew no limits. On the night of the betrayal all the disciples fled except John and Peter. Peter followed afar off and soon denied his Lord. But John went boldly into the court of the high priest. John alone of the disciples was found at the foot of the cross. Love begets love. Jesus must have known and appreciated the love that came to Him from John.

John was a man of temper and ambition. He had a great capacity for love. Jesus recognized these qualities in him. But none of these things explains the unique love which Jesus had for John. He must have loved John because of his spiritual sensitiveness. When the disciples failed to heal the demon-possessed boy while Jesus was on the mountain, Jesus said: "O faithless and perverse generation, how long shall I be with you, and suffer you?" (Luke 9:41.) We feel here the way in which the spiritual dullness of even His chosen disciples was almost intolerable to Jesus. John had a spiritual sensitiveness which meant that he could be very close to Jesus. We see this characteristic of John in his reaction to the empty tomb. When John entered the empty tomb and saw the linen cloth and the napkin folded separately, he immediately became aware of the tremendous significance of the thing which had happened. To the other followers of Jesus the empty tomb did not mean a word of hope. Mary Magadalene cries out: "They have taken away the Lord out of the sepulchre, and we know not where they have laid him." (John 20:2.) Peter leaves the tomb confused and uncertain. While Cleopas knows of the empty tomb he still speaks out of deep despair. But when John stands within the empty tomb he sees and believes. He does not know the whole story but he is confident that his Lord is alive. He knows that death has been conquered and that his Lord is the mighty Victor. Of course this faith of John receives powerful confirmation when the living Lord manifests Himself alive to John and the other disciples. But John counted the hour at which he first believed in the Resurrection as beginning not with the appearance of the risen Lord but with the inner certainty which came to him when he stood in the empty tomb.

This capacity to see the spiritual significance of the events of revelation was part of the peculiar fitness of John to be a witness to the things which Jesus said and did. The Gospel which bears his name was probably written late in his life. It may have received its final form from the hand of a younger disciple. This would explain the reference to John as the beloved disciple. But for its content it goes back to John. In John 21:24, he is identified as the disciple who wrote these things. The writer of the Fourth Gospel selects a limited number of incidents from the life of Jesus. In his narrative of them he speaks as an eyewitness. He tells the things he has seen and heard. He looks back on these events in the light of his knowledge of the Resurrection and against the background of his rich experience with the living Lord over many decades. With remarkable spiritual sensitiveness, he interprets the eternal significance of the things that Jesus did and said. He himself came to full belief in the risen Lord as he stood in the empty tomb, and he writes in order that those who read may believe that Jesus is the Christ, the Son of the living God, and that believing they may have life in His name. He records for us the way Jesus in His words to Thomas puts His blessing on those who have not seen and yet have believed.

The call of John to us is therefore first of all the call to faith. He himself has meditated over the meaning of the coming of God in Christ until he can say: "In the beginning was the Word, and the Word was with God, and the Word was God. . . . And the Word was made flesh, and dwelt among us, (and we beheld his glory, the glory as of the only begotten of the Father,) full of grace and truth." (John 1:1, 14.) He can add: "No man hath seen God at any time; the only begotten Son, which is in the bosom of the Father, he hath declared him." (John 1:18.) The Gospel of John traces both the development of faith and the hardening of unbelief. John knows that the call to faith is crucial. It is only as men believe in Jesus that they receive life in His name. John calls us to the faith that came to him as he stood in the empty tomb and saw and believed.

John is also the Apostle of Love. He has experienced the love of Jesus and he writes: "We love, because he first loved us." (1 John 4:19, R.S.V.) He says: "In this is love, not that we loved

God but that he loved us and sent his Son to be the expiation for our sins. Beloved, if God so loved us, we also ought to love one another." (1 John 4:10-11, R.S.V.) John became known as the disciple whom Jesus loved. Jesus knew the faith of John, the spiritual sensitiveness of John, the deep devotion which John gave. And John was very close to the heart of Jesus. John points us to a living Lord who would love us as He loved John. The Jesus to whom John bears witness calls us to faith and obedience. He asks us to share His compassion and to enter into the meaning of His sufferings. And as we respond to His call He is ready to claim us as beloved disciples and to set us to His tasks in our world.

> *"He that hath seen me hath seen the Father."—John 14:9.*

24. PHILIP

Scripture background: John 1:43-51; 6:5-7; 12:21-22; 14:1-12.

Philip is mentioned fifth in each of the four lists of the twelve apostles. (Matthew 10:2-4; Mark 3:16-19; Luke 6:14-16; Acts 1:13.) In each list he is the first apostle to be mentioned after the four familiar names, Peter and Andrew, James and John. Philip's home was in Bethsaida of Galilee. (John 1:44 and 12:21.) Jesus first found Philip in Judea on the day following His baptism. Probably Philip was among those from Galilee who had gone to Judea to hear John the Baptist. He and his friend Nathanael were watching and waiting for the coming of the long-expected Messiah. We have no record of the details of the scene in which Jesus called Philip. We do know that Jesus said to Philip, "Follow me." Philip accepted Jesus' invitation to become one of His disciples. He went out from his conversation with Jesus to tell Nathanael that he had found in Jesus of Nazareth, the son of Joseph, the One of whom Moses in the law and also the prophets had written.

When Nathanael was sure that nothing good could come out of Nazareth, Philip said to him, "Come and see." He brought Nathanael to Jesus in the firm assurance that Jesus would reveal Himself to his friend. Jesus did not disappoint him. Nathanael came to the conviction that Jesus was the Son of God, the king of Israel. Philip and Nathanael were with Jesus at Cana of Galilee. Beginning with the miracle at Cana, they were eyewitnesses of the mighty works through which Jesus revealed Himself to His contemporaries. Philip was with Jesus at the time of the feeding of the five thousand. He insisted that two hundred pennyworth of bread would not be enough to give each person a small helping. (John 6:7.) When the Greeks who had come up to the feast wanted to see Jesus they came to Philip. They may have selected him because he was the only one of the disciples with a Greek name. Philip found Andrew, and Andrew and Philip brought the request to Jesus. It was at this time that Jesus explained again to His disciples the necessity of His death. (John 12:20-25.)

Philip was with Jesus at the Last Supper. He heard Jesus say to His disciples: "I go to prepare a place for you. And if I go and prepare a place for you, I will come again, and receive you unto myself; that where I am, there ye may be also. And whither I go ye know, and the way ye know." (John 14:2-4.) He heard Thomas' question: "Lord, we know not whither thou goest; and how can we know the way?" He listened as Jesus answered: "I am the way, the truth, and the life: no man cometh unto the Father, but by me. If ye had known me, ye should have known my Father also: and from henceforth ye know him, and have seen him." It was at this point that Philip said to Jesus: "Lord, shew us the Father, and it sufficeth us."

In this request Philip gives expression to one of the deepest yearnings of the human heart. Philip wants a satisfying vision of God. He had come to believe in Jesus as the Christ, the Son of the living God. He had heard Jesus speak constantly of the Father in heaven. He asked Jesus before His departure to give His disciples a vision of the Father. He felt that such a vision would satisfy the unfulfilled longing of his heart. He is the spokesman for all those who would like to see their Maker face to face. Jesus answers Philip's request as He says: "Have I been so long time with you, and yet hast thou not known me, Philip? he that hath seen me hath seen the Father; and how sayest thou then, Shew us the Father?" (John 14:9.)

Jesus' answer to Philip is a tremendous statement which is filled with mystery. Here is One who sits at the table with His disciples and tells them that those who have seen Him have seen the Father in heaven. Can the eternal God be seen in One who walks as a man among men? Can it be that the vision of God comes to all mankind through One who was known as the carpenter, the son of Mary, of Nazareth? In Matthew 11:27, Jesus says: ". . . no one knows the Father except the Son and any one to whom the Son chooses to reveal him." (r.s.v.) We could be led here into some of the deepest questions of theology as we seek to understand the existence of the one God as Father, Son, and Holy Spirit. We could wonder what this statement does to all those who have sought God with no knowledge of Jesus Christ.

But while Jesus' statement can lead us into mystery and awe, it can also come to us as a profoundly simple answer to life's greatest question. Philip asks for a vision of the Father. Jesus replies: "He who has seen me has seen the Father." (r.s.v.) In his Prologue, John writes: "No one has even seen God; the only Son, who is in the bosom of the Father, he has made him known." (John 1:18, r.s.v.) As we see Jesus, we come to a true knowledge of the infinitely pure and holy Being who is the Creator and Sustainer of our universe.

Jesus reveals to us the Father in heaven who is concerned for all the needs of His children on earth. He says to us: "Are not two sparrows sold for a farthing? And one of them shall not fall on the ground without your Father. But the very hairs of your head are all numbered. Fear ye not therefore, ye are of more value than many sparrows." (Matthew 10:29-31.) We live in a world that often seems indifferent to moral and spiritual values, but Jesus says that at the heart of the universe there is One who knows and cares about the children of men.

The God who reveals Himself in Jesus is a Being of infinite

compassion. Jesus is marked at all times by unselfishness. He came not to be ministered unto but to minister. He gives Himself a ransom for others. He comes to seek and to save the lost. He offers sinners the forgiveness of God. He opens the way into the Kingdom of God for publicans and harlots. Even His wrath is rooted in His love for people, in His concern that every child of God shall attain his true destiny.

Jesus says: "He who has seen me has seen the Father." (John 14:9, R.S.V.) The attitudes of Jesus are the attitudes of God. As we see Jesus in the midst of our human life we have a revelation of the mind and heart of the Father. The God whom Jesus reveals has the capacity for wrath and judgment. In His condemnation of the hypocrisy of the scribes and Pharisees, Jesus speaks in scathing terms. We see in Him the wrath of God in the presence of hypocrisy and deceit. The wrath of Jesus is also revealed when He stands in the presence of the money changers in the Temple. Jesus in His own generation was a man of offense. He aroused the intense opposition of many of His contemporaries.

We can study Jesus in the various life situations which He faced, and we can know that His attitudes are a revelation of the attitude of God in similar situations today. When Jesus feels the ingratitude of the nine lepers who had no time to say "thank you," we can feel God's yearning for the gratitude of His children on earth. When Jesus speaks the great lament over Jerusalem we have a vision of the ache in the heart of God as His people refuse to come to Him. In the course of His earthly life, Jesus reveals to us the heart of God. We see in Him the wrath of God but we see also the love of God. John could say of Jesus: "having loved his own which were in the world, he loved them unto the end." (John 13:1.) Paul could speak of Jesus as "the Son of God, who loved me, and gave himself for me." (Galatians 2:20.) Jesus could say to Nicodemus: "God so loved the world, that he gave his only begotten Son, that whosoever believeth in him should not perish, but have everlasting life." (John 3:16.) And Paul could write to the Romans of "the love of God, which is in Christ Jesus our Lord." (Romans 8:39.)

The God who comes to us in Jesus Christ is not the God of

philosophy and speculation. He is the God who has acted in human history for man's redemption. The writer to the Hebrews can speak of the God who "brought again from the dead our Lord Jesus, that great shepherd of the sheep, through the blood of the everlasting covenant." (Hebrews 13:20.) In Jesus we see the God who has acted decisively for the salvation of mankind.

There is a note of amazement and wonder in Jesus' words as He says: "Have I been so long time with you, and yet hast thou not known me, Philip?" Philip had been with Jesus in many of the great moments of His life. He had seen the miracle at Cana of Galilee. He had been present at the feeding of the five thousand. He had heard Peter's confession at Caesarea Philippi. He had seen the power of God revealed through Jesus in miracles of healing. He had listened to the words of Jesus, who spake as never man spake. He had been with Jesus in those intimate hours when He was alone with His disciples. But Philip had failed to understand that he who had seen Jesus had seen the full and final revelation of the heart of God. If Jesus was amazed at Philip's failure to understand, must He not look at us with the same note of wonder and sorrow if we do not recognize Him—if we fail to understand that having seen Him we have seen the Father?

"Behold an Israelite indeed, in whom is no guile!"—John 1:47.

25. NATHANAEL

Scripture background: John 1:43-51; 21:2; Matthew 10:2-4; Mark 3:16-19; Luke 6:14-16; Acts 1:13.

The apostle whom John calls Nathanael is not mentioned by this name in any of the lists of the twelve apostles as given in the first three Gospels or in the book of Acts. Bartholomew is named as one of the apostles in each of the four times that the roll is given. In every instance he is mentioned in close association with Philip but nothing distinctive of him is recorded.

Most scholars feel that Bartholomew and Nathanael are different names for the same person. In a similar way, Peter is sometimes called Simon, and Matthew and Levi are identified as the same person. In addition to the story of the call of Nathanael which John gives us we learn in John 21:2 that Nathanael was from Cana of Galilee and that he was with six other disciples fishing in the Sea of Galilee when the risen Lord made Himself known unto them and served them a breakfast.

John tells us in his first chapter the story of the way in which Jesus, after His baptism, met with Peter and Andrew, James and John. The day following, as He was starting into Galilee, Jesus found Philip and said to him, "Follow me." We do not know anything of the contacts which preceded this call, and we have no account of the conversation which must have taken place between Jesus and Philip. We do know that Philip became convinced that he had found in Jesus the one "of whom Moses in the law, and the prophets, did write." (John 1:45.) As soon as Philip reached this conviction, he went in search of Nathanael. It is fair to assume that Philip and Nathanael were close friends and that as disciples of John they were watching and waiting for the coming of the Christ whom John had declared to be at hand. When Philip found Nathanael, he burst into the presence of his friend with the enthusiastic statement: "We have found him, of whom Moses in the law, and the prophets, did write." We can see Nathanael's enthusiasm awaken as his expression asks the questions: Who is He? Where is He? What sort of person is He? To his unspoken questions Philip answers: "Jesus of Nazareth, the son of Joseph." Nathanael's hopes fell. He lived in Cana of Galilee and he knew Nazareth. He was a plain, blunt man, and he expressed his sentiments with the cutting question: "Can there any good thing come out of Nazareth?" Nathanael could not believe that anything very worthwhile could originate in Nazareth. Certainly he was not prepared to believe that the long-expected Christ had been living all these years in Nazareth as the son of Joseph the carpenter.

Philip did not argue with Nathanael. He did not get into a

long debate concerning the people of Nazareth. He himself was convinced that Jesus was the Christ, and he was sure that if Nathanael would come to Jesus, Jesus could be trusted to reveal Himself to him. He said to Nathanael: "Come and see." Sometime the next day Philip and Nathanael caught up with the party. The meeting between Jesus and Nathanael may have taken place near Bethel, where God made Himself known to Jacob. As Philip and Nathanael come to Jesus, Nathanael is seeking the Christ but is unwilling to believe without adequate evidence. Philip is confident that Jesus will lead Nathanael from doubt to faith. Jesus sees Nathanael coming and turns to the other disciples and says: "Behold an Israelite indeed, in whom is no guile!" He reads the inner life of Nathanael and pays him a noble tribute. Nathanael responds to the tribute, but he cannot understand how Jesus, whom he has never seen before, can speak with such assurance of his basic integrity. He says to Him: "Whence knowest thou me?" Jesus answers: "Before that Philip called thee, when thou wast under the fig tree, I saw thee." This is the revelation of omniscience. Nathanael at once recognizes the statement as the sign which he was seeking. He says to Jesus: "Rabbi, thou art the Son of God; thou art the King of Israel." Nathanael's faith needed of course to be clarified. As a result of his discipleship with Jesus, he was to learn more clearly the meaning of the statement that Jesus was the Son of God, and the sense in which He was the King of Israel. Jesus indicates this as He says to Nathanael: "Because I said unto thee, I saw thee under the fig tree, believest thou? Thou shalt see greater things than these."

Nathanael stands at the beginning of that series of signs recorded for us in the Gospel of John through which Jesus led His disciples to a mature faith in Him. In concluding the conversation, Jesus says to Nathanael: "Hereafter ye shall see heaven open, and the angels of God ascending and descending upon the Son of man." (John 1:51.) The background of this statement is of course the revelation of God which was given to Jacob at Bethel. Jesus is saying that He as the Christ is in communion with

God, that He is the Mediator revealing God to men and bringing men to God.

When we ask concerning the trait of character which was outstanding in Nathanael we are led naturally to Jesus' words of him: "Behold an Israelite indeed, in whom is no guile!" Jesus means that because Nathanael is a true son of Israel he is free from all dependence on hypocrisy and deceit. This is true to the story of the changing of Jacob's name to Israel. Before Jacob met with God at Peniel his name had been Jacob, which means supplanter or trickster. Jacob had not been free from guile, but God gave him a new name, Israel, which means a prince with God. After this, he no longer dealt in deception. The spiritual sons of Israel would therefore be men who were free from guile. When the sons of Israel are not free from guile they are living as children of Jacob and not as the spiritual descendants of Israel. This truth was enforced by the whole of Israel's faith. The God of Israel is the God who demands truth of His followers. He does not permit His name to be used in connection with the oath which is not sincere.

This aspect of Israel's faith is reinforced in the revelation which came through Jesus. As Peter describes Jesus to the early Christians he says that Jesus "did no sin, neither was guile found in his mouth." (1 Peter 2:22.) Peter says that Jesus never used words to deceive anyone. Jesus said to Pilate: "To this end was I born, and for this cause came I into the world, that I should bear witness unto the truth. Every one that is of the truth heareth my voice." (John 18:37.) Jesus says of the devil: "He was a murderer from the beginning, and has nothing to do with the truth, because there is no truth in him. When he lies, he speaks according to his own nature, for he is a liar and the father of lies." (John 8:44, R.S.V.) According to Jesus, every lie is of the evil one. The temptation to speak falsely is to be branded as the voice of evil.

Paul writes to the Ephesians: "Wherefore putting away lying, speak every man truth with his neighbour: for we are members one of another." (Ephesians 4:25.) Paul knew that the lie always destroys confidence and that the building of the Christian community was impossible unless the Christians had a deep hatred of lying and were ready always to speak the truth every man to his neighbor. The truth is something that we owe to God. The Christian tells the truth because it is God's demand on him.

If we understand the meaning of our Christian faith we will so live that we are free from guile. While there are many aspects of this demand for truth, one of the temptations of our time is for men to seek to use the laws of psychology in the attempt to manipulate people. We seek to win friends and influence people in order that we may manipulate them to our advantage. There are some men who are so smart that they are not completely honest. You can never know just what they are trying to accomplish when they approach you. The demand for truth does not mean that we should lack tact and consideration for others, but it does mean that we should deal with people in a direct and straightforward manner.

In a similar way some people live behind a mask which they present to the world. The face they show to others does not genuinely reveal them. We do not have to seek to reveal the whole of our personality to every casual acquaintance, but we should seek to be our real selves. The Christian should not have to live behind a mask which conceals his true personality.

Jesus says: "Every one that is of the truth heareth my voice." (John 18:37.) It may seem to us that Nathanael came easily to the surrender of faith, but we must remember that before he came to Jesus he was an honest man who was seeking for the truth. He was ready to believe as soon as he received a sign which removed his doubts. On the other hand, if a man has dealt all his life in deceit, it is much more difficult for him to come to Jesus. The first law of the spiritual life is: "Never lie to God." But a man who has trusted in lies need not despair. He cannot at the same time be a follower of Jesus and a person who is filled with guile, but the God who changed Jacob can change him. If we come to Jesus confessing our false confidence in lies and asking to be cleansed from the temptation to deceive, we can receive from Him the power to become like Nathanael, an Israelite indeed, in whom there is no guile.

"I am the way, the truth, and the life: no man cometh unto the Father, but by me."—John 14:6.

26. THOMAS

Scripture background: Matthew 10:3; Mark 3:18; Luke 6:15; John 11:7-8, 16; 14:1-6; 20:24-31; 21:2; Acts 1:13.

Thomas was not present on that first Easter evening when the risen Lord revealed Himself to His disciples. Because of this absence, Thomas has been made the theme of countless sermons on church attendance. It is probably true that if Thomas had known what was going to happen he would have been found in his place with the rest of the apostles. One reason people fail to attend church services is that all too often there is lacking in such services the note of expectancy. Nothing is expected to happen and very often the expectation is fulfilled! We cannot reasonably expect a visible manifestation of the presence of the Lord at the services of worship in our churches today, but we do believe that the risen Lord is present with His assembled people and has the power to speak through some portion of the service His word to those who have gathered together to worship Him. The words which Jesus spoke to Thomas can be used by our Lord as the bearer of His message to men today.

Thomas is mentioned in each of the four lists of the twelve disciples, but the first three Gospels and the book of Acts give us no insight into what was distinctive in his personality. Thomas is known in the tradition of the Church as the bearer of the Gospel to Parthia and Persia, and the Church in India claims to go back to him. We cannot verify these traditions, but it is quite possible that Thomas was the first of the apostles to labor outside the bounds of the Roman Empire. Our concern at this time, however, is with Thomas when he followed Jesus as a member of the band of disciples.

John refers to Thomas as he tells the story of the raising of Lazarus. Jesus at the time was teaching at some point not too distant from Judea, possibly in Perea. A few weeks before this He had made a visit to Judea, and there the Jews attempted to stone Him. We know nothing of this visit apart from this incidental reference to it. We do not know why the Jews attempted to stone Jesus. And we do not know the details of the way He and His disciples avoided death at their hands. The experience had left in the minds of the disciples the feeling that a return to Judea would be dangerous. When Jesus says to them, "Let us go into Judea again," His disciples say to Him, "Master, the Jews of late sought to stone thee; and goest thou thither again?" (John 11:7-8.) When Jesus insists that He must go, Thomas says to his fellow disciples: "Let us also go, that we may die with him." Thomas reveals himself here as something of a pessimist, but he shows also a loyalty to Jesus which means that if necessary he is ready to face death with his Lord.

The next scene in which Thomas appears is on the night that Jesus was betrayed. The words of the fourteenth chapter of John are so familiar that we are apt to read them without grasping their tremendous meaning. Jesus knows that He stands at the end of the period of comradeship with His disciples in the days of His flesh. He knows that the time of His suffering and death is very near. He seeks in this conversation to prepare His disciples for His departure. The disciples on their part simply cannot believe that He whom they have acknowledged as the Christ is to be rejected and crucified.

In an effort to prepare them for the experiences which are ahead of them, Jesus says to His disciples: "Let not your heart be troubled: ye believe in God, believe also in me." He is urging them to believe in Him in spite of the events which are so soon to test their faith. He continues: "In my Father's house are many mansions: if it were not so, I would have told you. I go to prepare a place for you. And if I go and prepare a place for you, I will come again, and receive you unto myself; that where I am, there ye may be also." The word which is translated mansions means places of abode. It is, however, often used in the Greek to describe a home that is attractive. Jesus is telling His disciples that there is room for them in the Father's house. The Revised Standard Version translates verse 2, "In my Father's house are many rooms; if it were not so, would I have told you that I go to prepare a place for you?" The translation does not change the basic meaning of the passage. Jesus tells His disciples of a heavenly home in which there is room for them all. He says that He is going to prepare a place for them. He promises to come again and to receive them unto Himself.

We should not let the simplicity of the language obscure the importance of these promises. In them the Son of God is telling us of the Father's home. He is promising to take His loved ones to the place which He has prepared for them. He continues: "And whither I go ye know, and the way ye know." Probably Jesus is thinking here of something He has already said. The reference may be to His statement at the Lord's Supper in which His death is set forth as the basis of the New Covenant. But Thomas does not understand. He says: "Lord, we know not whither thou goest; and how can we know the way?" The question implied in the words of Thomas is one of the great questions of mankind. Can we believe that beyond this present life there is the Father's house? If there is a heavenly home in which there is room for us all, how can we get to it? Man, the mortal, can ask no more fundamental question.

Jesus answers: "I am the way, the truth, and the life: no man cometh unto the Father, but by me." (John 14:6.) "I am the way . . . no man cometh unto the Father, but by me." This may mean that the revelation of the heart of the Father is to be found in the Son. In the ninth verse Jesus states this as His answer to Philip. It may mean also the promise of Jesus to meet us in the hour of death and lead us to the Father's house. "I am the truth." This is the affirmation of Jesus that He Himself is the answer to the question of ultimate reality. At the heart of our universe there is a Living Person who reveals Himself to us in Jesus Christ.

He is the Creator of life. As Paul says: "All things were created

by him, and for him." (Colossians 1:16.) Jesus says, "I am the
life." (John 11:25.) Jesus Himself is the giver of life. He is the
giver of everlasting life. The Father has given Him the power to
give eternal life to those who come to Him. (John 17:2.)

We cannot fathom the depths of the answer of Jesus to the
question of Thomas. For a time the heart of Thomas must have
rested in the words of his Lord. But the events of the next twenty-
four hours shook his faith to its foundations. He was present when
Judas came with the armed band from the chief priests. He joined
his fellow disciples in the flight into the night; yet he knew of the
events of the next day. He must have believed to the end that
Jesus would save Himself by some manifestation of His divine
power. But he lived to know that the lifeless body of his Lord had
been taken down from the cross and laid in a tomb. The faith of
Thomas passed into dull despair.

On Sunday morning Thomas must have heard the rumors of the
empty tomb, but the empty tomb did not mean to him a living
Lord. He even refused to believe the other apostles when they told
him that they had seen the Lord. Thomas is known as the doubting disciple, but his doubt is not the hardened unbelief of the
Pharisees. The Pharisees refused to believe because they did not
want to believe. They did not want to acknowledge a fact which,
if accepted, would change their whole way of life. The doubt of
Thomas is the doubt that can lead to the larger faith. Thomas
wants to believe, but he is not willing to risk his life on an illusion.
The burnt child dreads the fire. The man who has loved and been
betrayed is slow to love again. He who has seen faith turn to
despair is not quick to move out again in the way of faith. But
the risen Lord meets Thomas and gives him an assurance of the
resurrection that can never be shaken. The proof of the reality
of the Father's home is the vision of the risen Lord in His resurrection body. After this Thomas cannot doubt the reality of the
resurrection world of God. In the vision of the risen Christ,
Thomas penetrates behind the veil of flesh to the eternal world
of God. Henceforth he can live as one who waits for the Saviour
from heaven who can fashion anew the body of his humiliation,
that it may be like unto His own glorious body, according to the

mighty power whereby he is able to subdue all things unto Himself. (Philippians 3:21.) Thomas knows now the way to the Father's house.

Jesus' last words to Thomas are something of a rebuke. Thomas has seen and believed, but the blessing of Jesus rests on those who have not seen and yet have believed. In these words Jesus speaks through the experience of Thomas to the needs of men today. This beatitude is for us. The blessing of Jesus is on those who have not seen and yet have believed. They have a faith that goes beyond the faith of Thomas.

> *"I am not come to call the righteous, but sinners to repentance."—Matthew 9:13.*

27. MATTHEW

Scripture background: Matthew 9:9-13; 10:3; Mark 2:14-17; 3:18; Luke 5:27-32; 6:15.

We can be reasonably certain that the man who is called Matthew in Matthew 9:9 is to be identified with the person named Levi in Mark 2:14 and Luke 5:27 and 29. We are not given the explanation of the double name. The name Matthew may have been given him by Jesus even as the name Peter was given to Simon, the son of Jona. He is called Matthew in each of the four lists of the apostles. Mark tells us that he was the son of a man named Alphaeus. Another of the apostles is distinguished from James the son of Zebedee as James the son of Alphaeus, but there is no suggestion that Matthew and this James were brothers.

The first Gospel is known as the Gospel according to Matthew. Eusebius quotes from Papias, bishop of Hierapolis in Phrygia, who wrote about A.D. 140, as follows: "Matthew collected the *logia* (sayings, or oracles) in the Hebrew language, and each one interpreted them as he was able."* The author of the first Gospel

* From *The Westminster Bible Dictionary*, by John D. Davis, p. 384. Revised and rewritten by Henry Gehman. Copyright, 1944, The Westminster Press. Used by permission.

evidently wrote in Greek. He uses about ninety per cent of the Gospel of Mark. In addition he gives a number of the sayings of Jesus which are not recorded in Mark. The Sermon on the Mount is the most extensive of these discourses. Probably the author of this Gospel used as his major sources the Gospel of Mark and a Greek translation of the sayings of Jesus which Matthew had preserved. If this surmise is correct, it is proper to call this Gospel the Gospel according to Matthew, since much of that which is distinctive in it may have gone back to the record of Jesus' sayings which Matthew kept. Who can measure the contribution of the man who was used by God to preserve for all mankind many of the sayings of Jesus?

Matthew must have been a man of spiritual possibilities. This can be argued both from what he did become and from the fact that Jesus selected him to be one of the Twelve. We can be sure that Jesus chose with great care the men who were to be witnesses unto Him. When we first meet Matthew he is known as the publican. This means that he was a tax collector for either the Romans or Herod the Tetrarch. The collecting of taxes is an essential function of good government, but the publicans were thought of as Jews who had sold themselves to the enemies of their country. In many cases they misused their power to enrich themselves by exploiting their own people. Luke tells us that Matthew was rich enough to give a great feast. We are not far wrong if we think of him as a man with spiritual possibilities who had sold himself to work evil. We will not understand the story unless we realize that Matthew was an outcast from his own society and that he knew it.

Matthew must have had some contact with Jesus before that day when Jesus called him at the seat of custom. Probably he had heard Jesus preach. The words of Jesus may have come to him as the voice of conscience speaking in condemnation of the evil of his life. And the offer of the forgiveness of God which Jesus made to all who sincerely repented may have stirred in Matthew hope for deliverance from his slavery to evil.

Jesus came to Matthew the publican as he sat at the seat of

custom and said to him, "Follow me." This is the call of Jesus to Matthew. It is the experience in which Jesus meets Matthew with all His claims on Matthew's life. The call of Jesus to Matthew involved the call to repentance. This is shown by the saying of Jesus, "I came to call sinners to repentance." If Matthew was to follow Jesus he had to leave the seat of custom. Jesus does not move among publicans and sinners to condone their sin but to call them to repentance. We cannot combine the following of Jesus and the yielding of our life to evil.

Jesus offers Matthew a way out. He invites Matthew to become one of His followers, to join the band of disciples that He is training to carry on His work. We do a man a wrong when we condemn his sin but offer him no hope of redemption and no chance to find a place of acceptance within a believing community. Jesus showed tremendous faith in the spiritual possibilities hidden in the life of Matthew the publican when He invited Matthew to become one of His chosen band of disciples.

Matthew *arose* and followed Jesus. This is his response to the call of Jesus. The call of Jesus demands action on the part of those to whom it comes. It meant for Peter and Andrew the leaving of their nets to follow Him. It meant to Matthew walking away from the seat of custom never to return. The call is not complete until we translate response into action. It meant for Matthew getting up out of his seat, turning his back to his past, and moving out onto a road in which he acknowledged Jesus as Lord and Master.

The choice of Matthew as a disciple was not popular with Jesus' contemporaries. By this act, Jesus violated the whole pattern of Jewish society. Every society enforces its standards by casting out those who ignore them. There is no other way in which a society can uphold its group demands. Probably Matthew's call would have passed without immediate opposition if he had not followed up his joining Jesus' disciples by giving a great feast. Because Matthew was an outcast of Jewish society the only people who would accept an invitation to his home were those who with him had incurred the wrath of respectable people. Mat-

thew's party was made up of those who were the castaways of
polite society. But Jesus did not stay away from this kind of
party. He came with His disciples. They sat down with Matthew
and his friends. In almost all cultures, the readiness of people
to eat together in a social engagement is a symbol of the removal
of barriers. Even in the time of Joseph, the Egyptians did not eat
with the Hebrews, and at the time of Jesus patriotic Jews would
not eat with Gentiles or publicans or social outcasts. In accepting
this invitation, Jesus deliberately and publicly defied the established customs of Jewish society. We are not surprised, therefore,
when the scribes and Pharisees come to the disciples of Jesus with
the question: "How is it that he eateth and drinketh with publicans and sinners?" (Mark 2:16.)

The question of the Pharisees is brought to Jesus' attention. He
answers their criticism of Him with the statement: "They that
be whole need not a physician, but they that are sick. But go ye
and learn what that meaneth, I will have mercy, and not sacrifice: for I am not come to call the righteous, but sinners to repentance." (Matthew 9:12-13.) The opening part of his statement is a proverb which will be accepted by all. "They that be
whole need not a physician, but they that are sick." Of course
there is a place for the practice of preventive medicine. People
who are in good health need at times to go to doctors for physical
examinations, but it still remains true that doctors must deal with
sick people. Hospitals minister not to the well but to the sick.
Jesus uses this proverb to remind the scribes and Pharisees that
His message is addressed to sinners. The distinctive new thing
Jesus brought was association with publicans and sinners. This is
the Gospel and our hope.

Jesus does not by the use of this proverb pass any final judgment on the moral and spiritual condition of His critics. In a
similar situation He tells in the fifteenth chapter of Luke the
parable of the prodigal son. In this parable there are two lost boys.
The younger son is lost in the far country of sin. The elder son
is still living in the home of the father, but he is lost in the sins
of self-righteousness. The father goes out to both sons, but we

are never told whether the elder son comes in. Jesus' call is directed to sinners whether they are respectable or outcast. He did suggest that it might be easier for the publicans and harlots to find their way into the Kingdom of God than for the Pharisees. He here says that the Pharisees need to learn afresh the meaning of the word of the Lord through the prophet Hosea: "I desired mercy, and not sacrifice." (Matthew 9:13; Hosea 6:6.)

But the heart of Jesus' statement is in the words: "I am come to call sinners to repentance." This was the explanation of His association with publicans and sinners. He went to them and lived with them to call them to repentance. When Jesus called Matthew to repentance He gave expression to a deep yearning that was always in His heart. He came to seek and to save the lost. He came to call sinners to forsake the way of evil and turn to God in new obedience. This was at the center of His message. Everything else was in the periphery. As we get the full impact of Jesus' statement of the purpose of His coming, we are bound to ask: "Who is this who comes to call sinners to repentance?" The answer is that He is the Christ, the Son of the living God. He is God manifest in the flesh for the salvation of sinners. This means that the statement which Jesus makes of the purpose of His life is also the statement of the redemptive purpose of God which comes to us through Him. Jesus went to sinners where they were. He ate and drank with them that He might call them to repentance. God comes to us in Jesus Christ in the context of our earthly life that He may call us to a knowledge of our sin, to repentance and surrender. The purpose of God for us is accomplished when, like Matthew, we hear the call of Jesus and arise and follow Him.

"Have not I chosen you twelve . . . ?"—John 6:70.

28. JAMES THE SON OF ALPHAEUS

Scripture background: Matthew 10:3; Mark 3:18; Luke 6:15; Acts 1:13.

James, the son of Alphaeus, is the one man among the twelve apostles of whom we know nothing that is distinctive apart from the fact that he was called the son of Alphaeus to distinguish him from James the son of Zebedee. There is no question as to this man's place in the apostolic band. He is mentioned in each of the four places in which the names of the apostles are given. There are some hints which have given opportunity for conjectures. Judas, not Iscariot, is identified in Acts 1:13 as Judas of James. The King James Version supplies the word *brother,* and the Revised Standard Version calls him the *son* of James. Both versions are guessing, since there is no Greek word to guide us. Among the women who followed Jesus to the cross is a woman named Mary who is distinguished from Mary Magdalene as the mother of James and Joseph. (Matthew 27:56; Mark 15:40.) This Mary was also with the women who came to the sepulcher on Sunday morning. (Luke 24:10.) It is possible that she was the mother of James, son of Alphaeus, but here also we are dealing with conjecture and not established facts. The apostle Matthew, known also as Levi, is called the son of Alphaeus, but we can be reasonably certain that the Alphaeus referred to here was not the same person as the father of James. (Mark 2:14.) We know the name, James of Alphaeus, but we know nothing distinctive about the person.

At least James the son of Alphaeus has the distinction of being the apostle about whom nothing distinctive is known. In every group we have to have followers as well as leaders. The man who goes quietly about his task may be accomplishing his work as efficiently as the man who is always calling attention to himself. If James the son of Alphaeus did not achieve prominence in the apostolic band it is also true that he did not achieve notoriety. The name of Judas is known to all but it is known as a name of shame.

All that we know about James, son of Alphaeus, is that he was one of the Twelve. But in knowing this, we know many things about this otherwise unknown man. If, for example, it could be said of a man that he was a member of the Stonewall Brigade we would know a lot about him. We would know that he fought through the War Between the States under the command of Thomas J. Jackson. We would know that he took part in those forced marches which gave Jackson's famous brigade the name of the Foot Cavalry of the Confederacy. James of Alphaeus was one of the Twelve, and because we know nothing distinctive about him we can think of the experiences which he must have had as a member of the apostolic band.

Jesus had many followers, but He chose from them twelve men whom He named apostles. The number is significant. It is chosen to correspond with the number of the tribes of Israel. In the various lists of the tribes we find some variations but always the number is twelve. This is because twelve was the symbol of completeness. When we think of the twelve tribes of Israel we think of the complete Israel. In one prophetic passage Jesus thinks of the twelve apostles as the founders of the new order of the people of God even as the twelve patriarchs had been the founders of Israel. (Matthew 19:28; Luke 22:30.) When Judas proved unworthy of his office, the disciples felt immediately that they must fill the vacancy. They felt that to qualify for the office a man must have been with them from the start, beginning with the baptism of John, and have been a witness of the Resurrection. We are told that Matthias was chosen and that he was numbered with the apostles. (Acts 1:15-26.)

Jesus needed disciples to assist Him in the task of ministering to the multitudes that came to Him. From the beginning of His ministry He called men to become His followers, and at an early time in the Galilean ministry He appointed twelve whom He named apostles. We can judge the seriousness of this decision by the fact that Jesus spent the entire night before in prayer to God. (Luke 6:12.) The men whom Jesus chose were unlearned and ignorant men if judged by the standards of the chief priests. (Acts 4:13.) But they were sturdy Galilean peasants whom Jesus chose not only for what they were but for what they had the capacity to become. Mark tells us that He chose them that they might be with Him and that He might send them forth to preach. (Mark 3:14.)

Disciples are necessary to any man who is to make a profound impact upon his world. A man is not a leader if he does not have followers. Disciples were peculiarly necessary to Jesus since the period of His public ministry was to be limited to three years. As far as we know, Jesus left nothing in writing. His impact on future generations was to be made by the report of Him given by His followers. He needed, therefore, an intimate band of disciples whom He might train for the carrying on of His work.

Jesus loved these men. There were times when their slowness to understand must have tested His patience. When He came down from the Mount of Transfiguration to find the nine disciples (including James of Alphaeus) impotent in the presence of human need, He cried out, "O faithless and perverse generation, how long shall I be with you? How long shall I suffer you?" (Matthew 17:17.) We feel here how intolerable it must have been to Jesus at times to bear with the sin and frailty of His disciples. It must have tested His patience when, on the night of His betrayal, there was strife among the disciples as to who should be the greatest in the Kingdom of God. (Luke 22:24.) But He also said to them: "Ye are they which have continued with me in my temptations." (Luke 22:28.) We see here His loneliness and His yearning for comradeship in His hour of testing. He could say to His disciples: "This is my commandment, That ye love one another, as I have loved you. Greater love hath no man than this, that a man lay down his life for his friends. Ye are my friends, if ye do whatsoever I command you. Henceforth I call you not servants; for the servant knoweth not what his Lord doeth: but I have called you friends; for all things that I have heard of my father I have made known unto you." (John 15:12-15.)

As one of the Twelve, James the son of Alphaeus knew the experience of living intimately with the Son of God in the days of His flesh. We know that he responded to the call of Jesus in such a way that he had an assured place in the band of the apostles. In all the great experiences of life, the thing which goes on inside of a man is central. Judas lived through the same experiences as the other disciples and disintegrated as he hardened his heart. But James of Alphaeus proved worthy of the trust which Jesus placed in him when He chose him to be one of the Twelve.

When we look back upon the New Testament record the significance of the apostles is seen in two places. Peter expresses it when he says that the man who is to be qualified to be added to the band of apostles must be selected from those who "have companied with us all the time that the Lord Jesus went in and out among us, beginning from the baptism of John, unto that same day that he was taken up from us," and that he must be "ordained to be a witness with us of his resurrection." (Acts 1:21-22.) When men began to see the full significance of the life and death of Jesus of Nazareth they could turn for their information about His words and deeds to twelve honest men who had been with Him from the beginning. Those who would see Jesus in the midst of our earthly life must go back to the story which these men told.

But the supreme significance of the apostles is to be found in their witness to the Resurrection. When Peter said, "This Jesus hath God raised up," he could also turn to the other apostles and say, "Whereof we all are witnesses." (Acts 2:32.) Luke tells us that Jesus after His passion showed Himself alive to His apostles "by many infallible proofs, being seen of them forty days, and speaking of the things pertaining to the kingdom of God." (Acts 1:3.) In the giving of revelation there is the event which takes place in history and there is the interpretation of the significance of this event. James the son of Alphaeus knew Jesus in the days of His flesh. He stood also at the empty tomb and in the presence of the risen Lord. He received from Jesus the interpretation of the meaning of His death and resurrection. He stood with the other apostles as they proclaimed to all men the mighty acts of God which must remain as the foundation of the believing community in all ages.

"Lord, how is it that thou wilt manifest thyself unto us, and not unto the world?"—John 14:22.

29.   JUDAS, NOT ISCARIOT

Scripture background: John 14:18-24; Matthew 10:2-4; Mark 3:16-19; Luke 6:14-16; Acts 1:13.

The discourses which begin with the fourteenth chapter of John are dominated by the thought of the impending separation of Jesus and His disciples. This was the last of the conversations they were to have together in the days of His flesh. Within a few hours there would follow in rapid succession Gethsemane, the arrest, the trials, the crucifixion, and death. In less than twenty-four hours Jesus' body would be lying in the tomb.

To strengthen His disciples for this ordeal Jesus says to them: "I will not leave you comfortless: I will come to you. Yet a little while, and the world seeth me no more; but ye see me: because I live, ye shall live also. At that day ye shall know that I am in my Father, and ye in me, and I in you. He that hath my commandments, and keepeth them, he it is that loveth me: and he that loveth me shall be loved of my Father, and I will love him, and will manifest myself to him." (John 14:18-21.)

At this point one of the disciples interrupted Jesus with a question. Judas, not Iscariot, said unto him: "Lord, how is it that thou wilt manifest thyself unto us, and not unto the world?" We know very little about the man who asked this question. When we seek to harmonize our four lists of the twelve apostles we find that we must identify him with the apostle whom Matthew calls Lebbaeus and Mark calls Thaddaeus. In the two lists which Luke has given us, he is called Jude of James. This may mean that he was the son of a man named James. It is possible that he was the son of the James of Alphaeus who in each of the four lists is mentioned immediately before him.

This man carried the same name as the traitor. It was an honorable name which went back to the founder of the tribe of Judah. It was a name that more recently had been made glorious in Judean history by its association with Judas Maccabaeus, the great leader who had gained for his people independence from Syria. But in Christian history the name Judas became inevitably associated with the disciple who betrayed his Lord for thirty pieces of silver. John is careful to let us know that the Judas who asks this question is not the traitor. All his life this Judas must have faced the necessity of clearing himself from the associations that went with the name Judas.

The only time this apostle stands out as an individual is in the asking of this question. We can perceive the intensity of his feeling by the very fact that this man who usually remained silent came forth with a question. The question which he put to Jesus is one of the great questions. Judas wants to know how it is that Jesus will manifest Himself unto the disciples and not unto the world. The question arises out of the statements which Jesus has just made. He has said, "Yet a little while, and the world seeth me no more; but ye see me," and He has said, "I will manifest myself to him . . . that hath my commandments, and keepeth them."

When Jesus said, "Yet a little while, and the world seeth me no more," He made a statement that was literally true. Within a few hours He was to be pronounced dead; His body was to be laid in the tomb, and the world was to see Him no more. This was Thursday, and on Sunday morning there was to come the witness to the empty tomb. And very soon there was to appear a believing community which had at its core a number of men and women who were sure they had seen the risen Lord. Peter says: "Him

God raised up the third day, and shewed him openly; not to all the people, but unto witnesses chosen before of God, even to us, who did eat and drink with him after he rose from the dead." (Acts 10:40-41.) The vision of the risen Lord was given to the believing community but not to the unbelieving world.

The witness to the Resurrection was essential to the belief of the Church in the living Presence of her Lord. But when Jesus said: "He that hath my commandments, and keepeth them, he it is that loveth me ... and I will love him, and will manifest my-self to him," He was making a promise that went far beyond the experiences of a limited number of disciples in the forty days between the Resurrection and the Ascension. He was setting the spiritual conditions upon which He would reveal Himself to His followers in all ages. It was to this promise that the question of Judas was directed when he said: "Lord, how is it that thou wilt manifest thyself unto us, and not unto the world?" Jesus answered Judas by repeating in a slightly varied form the promise which He had just made. He said to Judas: "If a man love me, he will keep my words: and my Father will love him, and we will come unto him, and make our abode with him." (John 14:23.)

There are three conditions involved in this promise of Jesus to Judas. We must have His commandments, we must love Him, and we must obey Him. The first is expressed in the phrase, "he that hath my commandments." We can be thankful that the first disciples of Jesus have left us a written record of the things that Jesus did and said. We know, for example, that He told us to love our enemies; that He commanded us to love one another as He had loved us; and that He laid upon us the responsibility of being witnesses to Him to the ends of the earth. Those of us who live in a land in which the Church is established and the Word of the Lord is proclaimed can be thankful for the spiritual heritage which is ours. In that thanksgiving we must face our responsibility for bringing all men to the place of discipleship to Jesus, a re-sponsibility which involves also the obligation to teach them to observe the things which He has commanded.

Jesus says: "If a man *love* me, he will keep my words." The followers of Jesus receive His commandments as the will of One who loves them and gives Himself for them. They are conscious of who Jesus is and of what He does for them. When they are confronted by Jesus, they respond to Him in love. The good comes to them, therefore, as the will of their Lord for them. Such an attitude toward the moral code was not unknown in the Old Testament. Joseph understood this when, in the time of temptation, he said: "How then can I do this great wickedness, and sin against God?" (Genesis 39:9.) David knew it when he repented of his sin with Bathsheba by saying to his God, "Against thee, thee only, have I sinned, and done this evil in thy sight: that thou mightest be justified when thou speakest." (Psalm 51:4.) But this understanding of the moral order as the expression of the personal will of the Lord who confronted them in decision and judgment was very real with those who had known Jesus in the days of His flesh. They had His commandments. They were under obligation to keep them because they were the expression of the righteous will of One whom they had known and loved. They knew, too, that Jesus loved them and that His commandments were given in love and understanding. The promise is to those who love Jesus.

We need to *know* the commandments of Jesus. We need to seek to know them because we love Him. But we need most of all to know the meaning of *obedience*. Obedience is the road to spiritual knowledge. In another place, Jesus says to the Jews: "My doctrine is not mine, but his that sent me. If any man will *do* his will, he shall know of the doctrine, whether it be of God, or whether I speak of myself." (John 7:16-17.) Our readiness to keep the commandments of Jesus is the test of the genuineness of our love for Him. Jesus says to Judas, not Iscariot: "He that loveth me not keepeth not my sayings." (John 14:24.)

The question which Judas put is very vital today. There are some people to whom Jesus is a great reality. He has given them their knowledge of God and their knowledge of the way of salvation. He has given them the hope of passing through death to the resurrection world of God. He has rescued their lives from futility and has given them the consciousness of His spiritual presence with them in the midst of the difficulties of life.

He has kept for them the promise made to the believing community in the beginning: "And, lo, I am with you alway, even unto the end of the world." (Matthew 28:20.) To those who have received Him, He has become the wisdom of God and the power of God; but to others the message of the Gospel remains foolishness or a stumbling block. We ask again the words of Judas, "Lord, how is it that thou wilt manifest thyself unto us, and not unto the world?" And we receive the words of the Lord in which He promises to manifest Himself to the man who has His commandments and loves Him and keeps His commandments.

We cannot control this experience. We are not able to manipulate it to suit our convenience. Our living Lord chooses the time, the place, and the manner in which He makes Himself known to His followers. But we know that He has promised to come and live in the hearts of those who have His commandments and who love and obey Him. If we meet the conditions which He has set, we can look to Him to make Himself known to us.

"Be not overcome of evil, but overcome evil with good."—Romans 12:21.

30. SIMON THE ZEALOT

Scripture background: Matthew 5:39-48; 10:4; Mark 3:18; Luke 6:15; Acts 1:13.

They called him Simon the Zealot. It was necessary to make an addition to his name to distinguish him from Simon Peter. This apostle is named each time the roll of the apostles is given. Luke calls him the Zealot. Matthew and Mark call him the Cananaean. In the King James Version this is translated the Canaanite. He was probably not a Canaanite. The word used here may be an Aramaic equivalent of the Greek word Zealot. It is therefore quite possible that this apostle at one time may have been associated with a Jewish party known as the Zealots. "The party was a movement started by Judas the Galilean in the time of Cyrenius to resist Roman aggression. Its increasing fanaticism contributed to provoke the Roman war. Ultimately it degenerated into a body of mere assassins, called Sicarii."*

We cannot be sure that Jesus' disciple who was called the Zealot had been associated with this party in Judaism, but the name would suggest this. Whether or not this implication is correct, the contrast between the way of life represented by the Zealots and by Jesus of Nazareth remains. There was something to be said for the Zealots. They represented one answer of a patriotic Jew to the Roman aggression. The publicans were traitors who were willing to sell themselves to Rome and to grow rich off the misery of their countrymen as they collected taxes for the foreign oppressor. The Sadducees struck a cynical bargain with the Roman leaders and were supported in their power by the Roman army. One of the fears of the chief priests and the Pharisees was that the movement led by Jesus would provoke the Romans to "come and take away both our place and nation." (John 11:48.) The Essenes became a community devoted to personal piety and the avoidance of political responsibility. In this situation the Zealots became a kind of secret society among the Jews. They were dedicated to the use of violence and terrorism. In particular their wrath fell upon the Jews who collaborated with Rome. It is interesting, therefore, to find in the intimate band of disciples Matthew the publican and Simon the Zealot. As in all groups of this kind, the way of the Zealots was open to terrible abuse. In the end they became guilty of acts of inexcusable brutality and cruelty, although many of those who joined them in the beginning may have done so as an expression of their Jewish patriotism.

The way of the Zealots is with us in the modern world. Underground resistance movements behind the Iron Curtain are an expression of this type of reaction to tyranny. No one would

* From *The Westminster Bible Dictionary*, p. 648. For an interesting study of the Zealots see Oscar Cullmann's *The State in the New Testament*.

defend all the deeds of terror which are done in such movements, but we can see in them a protest of those who feel that they are the victims of injustice. Whenever social tensions become acute there are apt to be those on both sides of the conflict who feel that they must resort to violence, to falsehoods, to terrorism, to fear, and to hatred.

Jesus saw in Simon the Zealot the spiritual possibilities of an apostle. His faith in this man was confirmed, for in the end he took his undisputed place as a faithful witness to his Lord. But when Simon the Zealot first came to hear Jesus of Nazareth preach, two conflicting ways of life met. What did Jesus have to say to this disciple and through him to all who would put their trust in the way of violence and terrorism?

Jesus was not willing to be the kind of Messiah that Simon the Zealot and those associated with him were expecting. The Zealots would have welcomed and probably were waiting for a Messiah who was willing to become the leader of an armed rebellion against Rome. But Jesus did not come to be a political deliverer; He came to save His people from their sins. He knew that there was no slavery like the bondage of a man to his own sins. He came to proclaim the forgiveness of God, to break the power of sin in the lives of men, and to lead His followers to lives of victory in their struggle with the power of evil in their own lives. The redemption of the individual is basic to the salvation of society. We cannot have Christian action unless we first have Christians.

Although Jesus Himself did not deal in violence, it does not follow that He would condemn all use of force by officers of the law. He recognized the Roman centurion as a man under authority and found in him a faith He had not found in Israel. (Matthew 8:10.) In a realistic understanding of our world there must be a place for the magistrate who bears the sword, and deeply as we would deplore war in either its ancient or its modern forms we cannot feel that all use of war power by the state is wrong. Peter did not require Cornelius to give up his commission when he received him into the Christian Church. The Holy Spirit must have fallen upon him while he was still a centurion.

It is necessary to go one step further and say that we cannot on all occasions condemn the right of revolution. If the existing state has lost all resemblance to the just state which is pictured in Romans, it may be necessary for men to raise in protest a standard to which the wise and righteous may repair. There is a difference between this kind of rebellion and personal retaliation.

But when these qualifications have been made, the contrast between the way of Jesus and the way of the Zealot remains. In the Sermon on the Mount, Jesus taught nonresistance to evil. He was dealing here with the old law of vengeance which prescribed an eye for an eye and a tooth for a tooth. Jesus insists that instead of dealing in vengeance we should return good for evil. A typical example was the right of a Roman soldier to require a Jew to carry his pack one mile. The Jew also had his rights, for the Roman soldier could not command him to carry the load for more than a mile. But Jesus says that if one mile is commanded we should go the second mile voluntarily. In so doing we undercut the whole atmosphere of tension and hate. If we walk the first mile as enemies we are apt to walk the second mile as friends. We go the second mile when we do willingly more than is demanded of us. We go the second mile when we refuse to avenge ourselves, and seek to overcome evil with good.

It is appropriate, therefore, that Jesus should follow His treatment of the law of vengeance with the passage in which He tells His followers to love their enemies, to do good to those that hate them, and to pray for those who despitefully use them and persecute them. He exemplified this teaching in His own life. In the midst of His sufferings on the cross He prayed for those who were crucifying Him. (Luke 23:34.) And Stephen, the first Christian martyr, faced his murderers with the prayer, "Lord, lay not this sin to their charge." (Acts 7:60.)

This teaching of Jesus can become real in the life of each individual Christian as he faces the evil around him. He can refuse to meet evil with evil. He can be unwilling to let hatred enter his soul. He can stand ready at all times to forgive those who have wronged him. He can seek the good of his enemy. This is the way of Jesus of Nazareth as contrasted with the way of the Zealot.

A program of passive resistance within the framework of respect for law and order can be forged into a powerful political weapon in the struggle for justice. Gandhi, for example, used nonviolent methods in his struggle to win independence for India. In this method, the one who challenges injustice takes upon himself the suffering involved instead of seeking to inflict suffering on his enemy. Such a method is most likely to succeed where there is the opportunity for a minority group to appeal to an enlightened Christian conscience. Many of those who have entered into this type of protest against evil have felt that in so doing they were walking in the way of Jesus of Nazareth.

The way of the Zealot is apt to bring moral deterioriation to those who practice it. This was true in the experience of the Zealot party in the time of Jesus. Those who joined the movement in the beginning may have been true patriots, but in the end the Zealots became lawless assassins who, by their terrorism, were partly responsible for bringing on the Roman war which resulted in the destruction of the Jewish nation. It was Jesus who said that those who take the sword will perish with the sword. (Matthew 26:52.) He wept over Jerusalem because she knew not the things which belonged to her peace. (Luke 19:42.) In contrast, those who fight with spiritual weapons will find that they grow in moral fiber and spiritual power. It was Jesus who said to His followers: "Blessed are they which are persecuted for righteousness' sake: for theirs is the kingdom of heaven." (Matthew 5:10.) This was the message of Jesus of Nazareth to Simon the Zealot.

"Who also betrayed him."—Matthew 10:4.
"To take the place in this ministry and apostleship from which Judas turned aside, to go to his own place."—Acts 1:25, R.S.V.

31. JUDAS ISCARIOT

Scripture background: Matthew 26:14-16, 20-25, 47-56; 27:3-10; Mark 14:10-11, 17-21; Luke 22:3-6, 47-53; John 6:70-71; 12:1-8; 17:12; 18:1-11; Acts 1:15-26.

In nine of the references to Judas in the New Testament, we are told that he was one of the Twelve. The writers of the New Testament were profoundly shocked by the fact that Jesus was betrayed by a member of the band of twelve disciples. Jesus must have chosen Judas as one of His disciples because He saw in him possibilities of spiritual development. Jesus would not have selected him if He had not known that Judas had the capacity to become one of His apostles.

Judas lived for three years in intimate association with the Son of God in the days of His flesh. He accompanied Jesus on many of His journeys through Palestine. He heard Jesus' teaching in precept and in parable. He was an eyewitness of the mighty works which God wrought through Him. He participated in the group processes through which the Twelve were trained for their task. He carried on a ministry of preaching and healing in the name of Jesus. But Judas steadily disintegrated in character. The reference to Judas in John 6:70-71 indicates that Jesus who had seen his spiritual capacities was aware also of the possibilities of evil in him. The reference to Judas in John 17:12 shows that Jesus felt keenly the failure of Judas to respond to His message.

The experience of Judas shows that the crucial thing in any man's life is his inner response to the things which life brings him. We would not underestimate the importance of environment. We know the value of the right kind of atmosphere. We would admit that in a limited sense there can be controlled situations. But the decisive thing in a man's destiny is his own response to the experiences he faces.

We know that Judas became the treasurer of the band of disciples. (John 12:6.) Incidentally, this shows that the disciples had a common fund from which they paid for their necessities and that on occasions there was enough surplus in the fund to provide gifts to the poor. The selection of Judas as treasurer indicates the confidence of the other disciples in his integrity and ability. Judas probably began with petty thieving. John insists that his objection to the extravagance of Mary of Bethany was not that he cared for the poor but that he was a thief and carried the bag. We are not completely surprised, therefore, when the avarice of Judas becomes a factor in his betrayal of his Lord.

At some time during Passion Week, Jesus' enemies reached the conclusion that He must be put to death. They decided also that it would not be wise to arrest Him during the feast. Jesus was still popular with the common people, especially those from Galilee, and the Messianic expectancy was at white heat. An ill-timed move on the part of the authorities might easily have provoked a Messianic revolt.

This dilemma created the opportunity which Judas sought. He went to the chief priests and asked them what they would give him if he would deliver Jesus unto them. They settled on thirty pieces of silver, which according to the Mosaic law was the approximate price of a slave in the market. Judas agreed to lead the chief priests to Jesus at a time when He could be seized apart from the crowd. Why did Judas enter into this bargain with the chief priests? A contributing factor was his love of money. He had come to the place where there was nothing he would not do for money.

But he must have had a deeper reason than this. He probably had accepted the invitation of Jesus to join the band of disciples in the hope of becoming part of a small popular movement and moving with it into a position of power. He was probably experiencing at this time a profound sense of disillusionment about the kind of Messiah that Jesus promised to be. Judas wanted to follow a world-conquering Messiah, not the Suffering Servant. But no considerations of this kind should weaken the impact of the simple statement that Judas, who was one of the Twelve, betrayed his Lord. Upon him there hangs the ignominy of the word "traitor." Even when we deal with thieves we view with peculiar disgust the man who squeals on his companions in crime. With how much greater loathing must we think of the man who betrayed the noblest Man who ever lived into the hands of those who sought His life?

With Judas there was the crucial period between the promise to deliver up his Lord and the actual performance of the deed. It was during this time that he sat with Jesus and the other disciples in what proved to be their last meal together. The conversation concerning the traitor which takes place at this meal should be interpreted as Jesus' last effort to save Judas. Jesus must have been deeply hurt that the traitor was found among the Twelve. He appeals to the law of hospitality as He reminds Judas that they have eaten bread together. And He solemnly warns Judas of the consequences of his deed as He says: "The Son of man goeth as it is written of him: but woe unto that man by whom the Son of man is betrayed! it had been good for that man if he had not been born." (Matthew 26:24.) Jesus never fails to emphasize the human responsibility of all the actors in the scenes leading to His death. Neither Pilate nor Herod, Caiaphas nor Judas, can avoid their responsbility for their sinful acts.

The appeal of Jesus is disregarded, and later in the night Judas appears in the Garden of Gethsemane with a band of soldiers sent by the chief priests to arrest Jesus. We do not have to tell again the familiar story, but we do need to pause for a moment on the sign of identification. It was night, and there were twelve men. A sign was needed that could not be mistaken. Judas told the soldiers to seize the man he kissed. And the kiss of Judas has ever since been the symbol of treachery.

The deed of Judas was done. It was followed quickly by remorse. Judas was not without a conscience, and the violence which he had done to his whole moral nature brought to him an overwhelming sense of guilt. This feeling of guilt deepened as he realized in the morning that his Lord was condemned to be crucified. The scene in which he returns the money to the chief priests is one that we can never forget. At least Judas was a better man than the men he dealt with. He had a sense of guilt, whereas they seemed completely hardened. It is strangely ironic that they are anxious not to misuse the money which is the price of blood, although they have no conscience about putting an innocent man to death. Judas stands out in this scene as a man who knows remorse but does not know repentance unto life. He does not turn to Jesus for the forgiveness he would have received if he had asked for it.

We do not know enough to harmonize completely the two accounts of Judas' death. It is clear that he died a suicide. His last act was the act of his own destruction.

What was the final end of Judas? The tragedy of his life is expressed in the reference to him in Acts. He was chosen by Jesus for a place among the twelve apostles. He could have been one of the men through whom Jesus laid the foundations of His Church. He could have looked forward beyond death to the place which Jesus said He was going to prepare for His disciples. But Judas turned aside in the hour of crisis and fell from the ministry and apostleship to which he was chosen. Those who had been his companions say of him that he turned aside to go to his own place. He turned away from Christ, and Satan entered into him. He left the fellowship of the apostles to join the ranks of the traitors. Jesus says of him that it would have been better for that man if he had never been born.

We are not called like Judas to be apostles. We are called to be disciples. We have the privilege of acknowledging Jesus as Lord and Master. He calls us to an eternal destiny. We should learn from the experience of Judas the utter tragedy of turning aside from our high calling to miss our destiny and go to our own place.

Faces of the Passion Week

"Jesus answered him, I spake openly to the world; I ever taught in the synagogue, and in the temple, whither the Jews always resort; and in secret have I said nothing."—John 18:20-21.

32. ANNAS

Scripture background: Luke 3:2; John 18:13, 19-24; Acts 4:6.

When Jesus was arrested in the Garden of Gethsemane, He was bound and led at once to Annas, the high priest. This was the first of three stages in His trial before the Jews. It was not a trial in the strictest sense of the word. No witnesses were called, and no specific charges were made against Him. After Annas had completed his examination, he sent Jesus bound to Caiaphas. There followed the trial before the Sanhedrin which is described for us in Matthew 26:57-68 and Mark 14:55-65. This trial was probably held after midnight and was therefore illegal, but as a result of it the leaders of the Jews reached a consensus in which they found Jesus guilty of blasphemy and condemned Him to death. It was followed by an early morning trial which is mentioned in Luke 22:66-71. At this time, the decision reached the night before was confirmed and a strategy was worked out for presenting the case to Pilate. Our concern in this study is exclusively with the examination before Annas.

The Annas who is referred to here is known to us in secular history. He was high priest from A.D. 7 to A.D. 14. After he was deposed by Valerius Gratus, the predecessor to Pilate, he continued to rule behind the scenes through his son Eleazar, who was high priest for a brief time, and through his son-in-law, Joseph

surnamed Caiaphas, who held office A.D. 18-36. After Caiaphas
was deposed, four more sons of Annas succeeded him. The last of
these, who was also named Annas, was responsible for the death
of James, the brother of our Lord. It is obvious that Annas retained great influence during a crucial period in Jewish history.
The Gospel writers consistently refer to him as high priest and
at the same time recognize Caiaphas as high priest.*

Annas appears at various places in the New Testament record.
Luke says that the word of God came to John the Baptist when
Annas and Caiaphas were the high priests. John supplements the
accounts of the trial of Jesus in the first three Gospels with the
story of the investigation conducted by Annas. Annas and Caiaphas are both present when Peter and John face the assembled
Sanhedrin a few months after the death of Jesus. In Peter's speech
at this time, Annas hears the apostles' witness to the resurrection
of Jesus. The career of Annas was possible only to a man who was
a master of ecclesiastical diplomacy. The references to him both
in secular history and in Scripture point to a man steeped in
cunning and intrigue. This is the man to whom Jesus was sent
first.

The purpose of Annas was to entrap Jesus in His words. He
sought to lead Him to say something that could be used effectively
against Him. In this battle of wits, Jesus, who had put to silence
the Herodians, the Sadducees, and the Pharisees, was not to be
caught by Annas. The high priest asked Jesus of His teachings
and of His disciples. Jesus replied: "I have spoken openly to the
world; I have always taught in synagogues and in the temple,
where all Jews come together; I have said nothing secretly. Why
do you ask me? Ask those who have heard me, what I said to
them; they know what I said." (John 18:20-21, R.S.V.)

This answer defeats the purpose of Annas. Jesus has said nothing that he can take hold of. He has not given the high priest any
material he can produce in the trial which is to follow. Jesus'
words also reveal the hypocrisy of Annas. The questions of the
high priest are not honest questions. He is not seeking for true information concerning Jesus or His disciples. If he had really

---

* Plummer, *The International Critical Commentary on Luke*, p. 84.

desired to become familiar with the teachings of Jesus he had had
abundant opportunity. Jesus' reply is remarkable most of all for
its boldness. The way it affected those who stood by is revealed in
the action of one of the officers. This man struck Jesus with the
palm of his hand, saying, "Is that how you answer the high priest?"
(John 18:22, R.S.V.) He must have felt that the high priest had not
been shown proper respect, but we cannot excuse this officer for
his act of violence. And we cannot excuse Annas, who acted as
high priest and permitted one of his men to strike a prisoner who
had not been judged. Paul in a similar situation condemned the
high priest in no uncertain terms for his failure to enforce the
law he was sworn to uphold. (Acts 23:3.) We cannot but marvel
at Jesus' composure here. He said to the man: "If I have spoken
wrongly, bear witness to the wrong; but if I have spoken rightly,
why do you strike me?" (John 18:23, R.S.V.) We do not know
Annas' reaction to this scene, but we do know that when Peter
and John, whom he considered unlearned and ignorant men,
spoke boldly in his presence, he was among those who remembered that these men had been with Jesus.

Jesus' words to Annas are a description of the way in which He
carried on His ministry. He spoke openly to the world. He taught
in the synagogues and in the Temple where the Jews always re-
sorted. When the synagogues were closed to Him, He spoke
openly in the streets. He had no secret places of meeting. He had
no secret doctrine for the initiated which was kept from the
public. The statements Jesus makes here are not inconsistent with
His ministry in the training of the Twelve. There are areas of
truth which can be apprehended only by those who are committed to the truth. Even Nicodemus was not prepared to understand
the deep things of God. But Jesus' approach was consistently
open and aboveboard. He had no secret teachings. He had no
concealed motives. In all of this, Jesus stands in strong contrast to
Annas. Annas is the master of intrigue. He cannot understand a
man who deals always in the open.

From this point of view the enemies of Jesus pay tribute to
His transparent honesty. When the Herodians come to entrap
Him in His talk they say: "Teacher, we know that you are true,

and care for no man; for you do not regard the position of men, but truly teach the way of God." (Mark 12:14, R.S.V.) These words are spoken in flattery. They are full of guile. But they are true; for once it suited the purpose of Jesus' enemies to tell the truth. But the poorly concealed cunning of the enemies of Jesus stands out in sharp contrast with the integrity of His own life. The way Jesus carried on His work was rooted in His respect for the truth.

The example of Jesus makes demands on those who would follow Him. John writes: "This then is the message which we have heard of him, and declare unto you, that God is light, and in him is no darkness at all. If we say that we have fellowship with him, and walk in darkness, we lie, and do not the truth: but if we walk in the light, as he is in the light, we have fellowship one with another." (1 John 1:5-7.) Without attempting an exhaustive interpretation of this passage, we can say that John points to Jesus as one who walked always in the light and says that those who follow Him should walk in the light as He is in the light.

This is an attitude which should mark all those who seek to do the Lord's work. At times men who have held high positions in ecclesiastical hierarchies have been men of cunning and guile. And not all of those who have presented the Gospel message have consistently walked in the light as Jesus was in the light.

At this point Jesus might well speak a word to those who sit at the tables of the nations. Diplomacy has a tendency to become synonymous with intrigue and guile. Where there is no profound respect for the truth as God's demand on men, the representatives of nations may deal in falsehood if the lie seems to serve the best interests of their nation. The Communist line is usually determined by expediency rather than by regard for the truth. But the true Christian must deal always openly and aboveboard with a respect for the truth which cannot be violated.

John adds that when we walk in the light as Jesus is in the light we have fellowship one with another. There can be no abiding fellowship between men or nations which is not based on confidence, and there can be no enduring confidence when men seek to deal in falsehoods. We must continue to walk in the light if we are to have fellowship one with another.

Jesus stands before Annas. Annas has been the high priest. He is still the power behind the office. As the high priest he has administered the sacrificial system of Judaism. He himself must have known that the blood of bulls and goats could not take away sin. The value of the system which he administered was that it pointed forward to the great sacrifice that had to be made before sin could be pardoned. Now Annas stands in the presence of the One who has come to give His life a ransom for many. Annas is so steeped in guile that he is unable to recognize in the figure of the Person who stands before him the long-expected Deliverer. But John, who looks back on Jesus in the light of the Resurrection, knows that "the blood of Jesus Christ . . . cleanseth us from all sin." (1 John 1:7.) The high priest who is unworthy of his office faces the One who has come to make atonement for the sins of His people. But Annas does not penetrate the veil of flesh to the vision of the Son of God who has come to die for the sins of the world.

"He hath spoken blasphemy . . . He is guilty of death."
—Matthew 26:65-66.

33. CAIAPHAS

Scripture background: Matthew 26:57-68; Mark 14: 55-65; Luke 3:2; 22:63-71; John 11:47-54; 18:13-14, 19-28; Acts 4:6-28.

Joseph Caiaphas was appointed high priest about A.D. 18 by Valerius Gratus, the Roman procurator and immediate predecessor of Pontius Pilate. He continued in office until about A.D. 36 when he was deposed by Vitellius, the Roman president of Syria.* He was the son-in-law of Annas, who had been high priest

* Josephus, *Antiquities* xviii, 2-4. Dates obtained from Plummer, *The International Critical Commentary on Luke.*

before him. During part of this time Annas and Caiaphas were mentioned as serving jointly. (Luke 3:2.) Annas probably was consistently the power behind the throne. The high priest was thought of as the spiritual head of the Jewish people. The Romans allowed him to exercise also a considerable amount of temporal authority over his own people. Saul of Tarsus received from the high priest authority to go to Damascus and bring the Christians there bound to Jerusalem for trial. (Acts 9:1-2.) The office of the high priest was at times in the history of Israel held by noble men who were the true spiritual leaders of their people. Under the Roman domination it had become in part a political appointment which was given to men sadly lacking in the requisite spiritual qualifications for this high position. But the Jews continued to respect the office as the symbol of the religious leadership of their people.

John reminds us that Caiaphas was high priest in the year that Jesus made His final visit to Jerusalem. We cannot but wonder what might have happened if a different man had at this time held the exalted position of spiritual head of the Jewish people. Caiaphas was high priest, and as such he was responsible for the arrest of Jesus. He presided over the council when they pronounced Jesus guilty of blasphemy and sentenced Him to death.

The four Gospels describe for us both the development of faith and the hardening of unbelief. This is particularly evident in the Gospel of John. The writer of this Gospel has carefully selected his incidents in such a way that they reveal the deepening of faith in the followers of Jesus and the development of unbelief in the hearts of His enemies. He traces the hardness of heart, the spiritual blindness, which falls on those who reject Jesus.

Caiaphas was high priest when John began his ministry. He must have been among those who refused to accept John as a true prophet. Caiaphas could not have been ignorant of the appearance of Jesus of Nazareth, but the first time Caiaphas actually appears in the New Testament story is when those who have witnessed the resurrection of Lazarus go and tell the Pharisees. They in turn report to a meeting of the council which includes both

Pharisees and Sadducees. These leaders of the Jews admit that Jesus has performed many miracles. They feel that if they let Him alone all men will come to believe on Him. They are afraid that He will become the leader of a Messianic revolt which will bring swift and terrible judgment from Rome. While Jesus had no intention of leading this type of rebellion, we can understand their fears. Forty years later the Romans did come with an army "to take away their place and nation." In this setting, Caiaphas makes a speech in which he insists that it is better for one man to be put to death than for the whole nation to be destroyed. Caiaphas is confronted with the mighty works of Jesus. He does not ask whether or not these signs mean that Jesus is approved of God. Caiaphas is not interested in either truth or justice. His counsel is that of expediency. He is willing to sacrifice the life of one man who may be innocent to save the nation as a whole. In fact, he predicts that Jesus will die for the whole nation. As John looks back on this scene he sees in the words of the high priest an unconscious prophecy of the meaning of Jesus' death. The advice of Caiaphas prevails, and the council reaches the conclusion that Jesus must be put to death.

For a brief time Jesus remained more or less in seclusion, but at the beginning of the week before the Passover He went boldly to Jerusalem. Caiaphas and his advisers immediately began to plan to bring about His death. They decided, however, to wait until after the feast to avoid a scene when the multitude was present. The offer of Judas changed their plans. With his help, they arrested Jesus at night in the Garden of Gethsemane.

Caiaphas' plans included a quick decision by the Sanhedrin, the highest court of the Jews. This was to be followed by an appeal to Pilate for the sentence of crucifixion since the Jews at the time were not permitted to administer the death penalty. It is important to reflect here on the comparative guilt of the Romans and the Jews. Jesus says to Pilate: "Thou couldest have no power at all against me, except it were given thee from above: therefore he that delivered me unto thee hath the greater sin." (John 19:11.) Both Pilate and Caiaphas held their power as a trust from God.

Pilate abused his power by condemning to death a man whom he knew to be innocent. But Caiaphas presided over the highest court of the Jews when Jesus came unto His own and His own received Him not. It was under the leadership of Caiaphas that the Jews crucified their Messiah. Compared with Pilate, Caiaphas was guilty of the greater sin.

In the trial before Caiaphas, the enemies of Jesus first attempted to produce witnesses who would prove Jesus guilty of deeds that would justify the death sentence. This attempt broke down. It was at this time that Caiaphas ceased to be judge and became prosecutor. He said to Jesus: "I adjure thee by the living God, that thou tell us whether thou be the Christ, the Son of God." (Matthew 26:63.) The charge is reported with some variations in the other Gospels but its essential meaning is the same. The Christ stands in the presence of the highest court of His people. He must say whether or not He is indeed the Christ. According to Mark, Jesus answers: "I am: and ye shall see the Son of man sitting on the right hand of power, and coming in the clouds of heaven." (Mark 14:62.) When we put together the three passages in which this scene is reported, we can make the following comments: First, Jesus does not deny Himself. During His ministry He sought to avoid public use of the term "Christ" because His understanding of the term did not fit the popular expectations of the Messiah; but He never says that He is not the Christ. Second, it is clear that the Sanhedrin interpreted Jesus' answer as His assertion that He was the Christ. Third, in all three passages Jesus contrasts His present condition as the Suffering Servant on trial before His own people with His future glory. Those who are passing judgment on Him now see Him in His humiliation when His glory is veiled in the flesh. But Jesus predicts that they will live to see Him in His glory. At that time it will be a question not of their decision concerning Him but of His decision concerning them.

We need not be surprised that Caiaphas and his court found Jesus guilty of blasphemy and sentenced Him to death. From the beginning, the claims of Jesus had involved implications that would be blasphemous if false. This was true of the scene which marked the beginning of offense, when Jesus claimed to have power on earth to forgive sins. The Pharisees had said at the time: "Why doth this man thus speak blasphemies? Who can forgive sins but God only?" (Mark 2:7.) They had disagreed with Jesus on many subjects, such as His attitude toward the keeping of the Sabbath and His willingness to receive publicans and sinners, but always the basic offense was the implications of His claims. This is particularly true in John. In this Gospel, Jesus presents Himself as the light of the world. He claims to have been before Abraham. He says that He is the resurrection and the life and that He has power to raise the dead. When the chief priests make their case before Pilate they start out with the assertion that Jesus seeks to be the king of the Jews; that is, that He is a Zealot who is dangerous to Rome. But they are finally forced to give their real reason when they say: "We have a law, and by our law he ought to die, because he made himself the Son of God." (John 19:7.)

Caiaphas and the Sanhedrin are confronted by Jesus of Nazareth. They must decide concerning Him. He offers Himself as the Christ, the Son of God. If the leaders of the Jews accept these claims, they must yield themselves to Him as their long-expected Messiah. If they are convinced that His claims are false they must pronounce Him a blasphemer, one who according to their law is guilty of death. Their dilemma is stated simply. If the claims of Jesus are true, they must accept Him as the Christ. If His claims are false, they must reject Him as an imposter.

The failure to recognize the Christ was the culmination of a long period of deepening unbelief on the part of those who rejected Him. There are none so blind as those who will not see. The last picture we have of Caiaphas is when he stands in the presence of Peter and John. These men give to him their witness to the risen Lord. Their testimony is confirmed by a miracle which Caiaphas cannot deny. But all that Caiaphas can do is to command them "not to speak at all nor teach in the name of Jesus." (Acts 4:18.) This command they had no intention of obeying.

It is easy to sit in judgment on Caiaphas as we stand in the perspective of history. He failed to recognize the Son of God in the days of His flesh. Instead he took the lead in having Him condemned to death. But the dilemma of Caiaphas is faced in a somewhat different form by all who are confronted by Jesus of Nazareth. In the witness to Jesus preserved for us in the New Testament, there can be little doubt that He offered Himeslf as the Son of God, the Saviour of the world. We must face, as His contemporaries faced, the claims which He made for Himself. These claims are either true or false. If they are not true, they are the claims of a man who had grandiose delusions. If they are true, we must recognize the Son of God in the context of our earthly history and acknowledge Him as our Lord and Saviour.

> *"To this end was I born, and for this cause came I into the world, that I should bear witness unto the truth. Every one that is of the truth heareth my voice."—John 18:37.*

34. PONTIUS PILATE

Scripture background: Matthew 27:1-26; Mark 15: 1-15; Luke 23:1-25; John 18:28—19:42.

When Christians repeat the Apostles' Creed, they say, "suffered under Pontius Pilate." It is at this point that the Creed touches secular history. Pontius Pilate was the Roman governor of Judea who, in the year A.D. 30, condemned Jesus of Nazareth to death by crucifixion. The part which Pilate played in the death of Jesus was crucial. When the chief priests bring Jesus to him and ask for a sentence against Him, Pilate says to them: "Take ye him, and judge him according to your law." They reply: "It is not lawful for us to put any man to death." (John 18:31.) The Jews had a limited amount of self-government, but they were not permitted to pass the death sentence.

The Sanhedrin found Jesus guilty of blasphemy and judged Him to be worthy of death. If they had executed this sentence,

Jesus would have died at the hands of His own people by stoning. It was the Romans who crucified criminals. When Jesus was brought into Pilate's court it was necessary to frame a charge against Him which would have meaning for the Romans. Whereas He had previously been condemned for blasphemy, He was now accused of being a disturber of the peace and of making Himself a king. Pilate was immediately suspicious of these charges. The Jews were not in the habit of turning this type of political prisoner over to him for judgment. He soon realized that Jesus had been delivered up because of envy, and he was not long in reaching the conviction that this man was not a threat to Rome and was not guilty of any crime deserving imprisonment or death. At the same time, Pilate hesitated to release Jesus as he did not wish to offend needlessly the leaders of the people he had been sent to govern. Pilate is in the position of a man who would like to do the right thing but is tempted to do the expedient thing. He does not want to condemn an innocent man. He does not desire to violate truth and justice. But he does want to please the leaders of the Jews, and he is afraid of any report to Caesar which might bring about an investigation of his government.

In the effort to escape from this dilemma, Pilate has Jesus scourged and presents Him to the multitude in an appeal to their mercy. He hopes to get the mob to ask for Jesus rather than Barabbas. He seeks also to avoid a decision by sending Jesus to Herod. But all of his efforts to avoid making a responsible decision fail, and he must give judgment concerning Jesus.

God did not leave Pilate without a warning in the hour of his crucial decision. Before the day of the trial he may have heard some reports of the deeds of Jesus of Nazareth. We know from John that many of Jesus' miracles had been performed in Judea. Could Pilate have been completely ignorant of the stories with which Herod was quite familiar? As Pilate faced his prisoner he soon became conscious that he was not dealing with a typical leader of revolt. The majesty of Jesus' bearing must have impressed him. He was warned also by the message he received from his wife. (Matthew 27:19.) The sense of awe which Pilate had in dealing with this prisoner was deepened when the Jews said to him: "We have a law, and by our law he ought to die, because he made himself the Son of God." (John 19:7.) Pilate, with a show of power which reveals the fear at his heart, says to Jesus: "Speakest thou not unto me? knowest thou not that I have power to crucify thee, and have power to release thee?" (John 19:10.) And Jesus replies: "Thou couldest have no power at all against me, except it were given thee from above: therefore he that delivered me unto thee hath the greater sin." (John 19:11.) Jesus reminds Pilate that he is responsible to a higher Authority for the way he uses his power as a judge.

It is as Pilate is trying to decide whether to do the right thing or the expedient thing that we have the statement to Pilate in which Jesus most clearly reveals Himself. He says: "To this end was I born, and for this cause came I into the world, that I should bear witness unto the truth. Every one that is of the truth heareth my voice." (John 18:37.) This is one of Jesus' most significant statements. It should be set beside His words to Thomas, "I am the way, the truth, and the life: no man cometh unto the Father, but by me" (John 14:6); or His message to Philip, "He that hath seen me hath seen the Father" (John 14:9); or His saying at the Feast of Tabernacles, "I am the light of the world: he that followeth me shall not walk in darkness, but shall have the light of life" (John 8:12).

Truth can be defined as agreement with reality. In each of these statements Jesus is saying that He has come to reveal to man the ultimate nature of the universe in which he lives. He reveals the Father in heaven. He says that on the throne of our universe there is a personal God who loves us enough to send His Son to die for us. He is revealing to us the fact that the moral order of the universe is grounded in the will of a righteous God. He is revealing to man his capacity to become through faith a child of God. He is telling mortal man of a life beyond the grave in the many mansions which are in the Father's house. He is revealing Himself as the way of man's salvation. In Jesus Christ we face the One who has come into this world to bear witness to the truth.

When we acknowledge Jesus to be the One who came to bear witness to the truth we do not see at once what bearing His message about Himself has on Pilate's dilemma of choosing between the right thing and the expedient thing. But there is a close relation between the message of Jesus and the decision of Pilate. When a man faces the choice between the right thing and the expedient thing, his answer is certain to flow from his fundamental convictions about the meaning and purpose of life. In answer to Jesus' statement Pilate says somewhat contemptuously: "What is truth?" It is possible to live in a world in which we are not interested in the truth. We can lose the sense of a vital distinction between truth and falsehood. We can obscure the eternal difference between good and evil. We can ignore the existence of a moral order which cannot be violated with impunity. We can forget that the demand for justice grounds in the will of a righteous God. If we believe that we live in this kind of universe, Pilate's decision makes sense. If the universe is without purpose or meaning and if our human life is without eternal significance, then the expedient thing is probably the best guide to human conduct. But if we live in the world which Jesus Christ reveals, we must consistently seek to do the right regardless of the question of expediency.

It is difficult to condemn Pilate too severely if we judge him by the standards of political expediency. He had to look out for his own career. The religious leaders of the Jews wanted the death of this man. The real guilt was with them. Who could blame a Roman governor for sacrificing a man who was probably innocent to avoid offending too deeply men he had to work with? But if we look at this decision in the light of eternity we can see the fatal flaw in Pilate's reasoning. In the providence of God, he sat in the seat of justice when the Christ was on trial, and he misused his power as a judge to give the death sentence to the Son of God in the days of His flesh. The scene in which Pilate washes his hands and seeks to avoid the guilt which he knows is his bears witness to his own sense of violated justice.

Jesus gives His words a universal application when He says:

"Every one that is of the truth heareth my voice." Pilate failed to listen to Jesus because he had no real understanding of the difference between truth and falsehood. Nathanael came to a living faith because he was a man in whom there was no guile. If we consistently deal in deceit we come to the place at which there is in us a moral incompatibility to the truth. If we are committed at all times to following the truth as we see it, we are prepared to hear the word of the One who came to bear witness to the truth. Jesus has come to reveal to us the ultimate truth concerning God and man. He is the light of the world. He promises that those who follow Him shall not walk in darkness but shall have the light of life. But the condition of laying hold of the knowledge which Jesus can give is the willingness to receive the truth.

"He answered him nothing."—Luke 23:9.

35. HEROD ANTIPAS

Scripture background: Matthew 14:1-12; Mark 6:14-30; 8:15; Luke 3:1, 19-21; 9:7-9; 13:31-35; 23:7-12; Acts 4:27.

There are four Herods who are prominent in the narrative of Scripture. The first of these is, of course, Herod the Great. He was king of Judea from 37 B.C. to 4 B.C. In his effort to destroy the child who was born King of the Jews, he ordered all the male children under two years old in Bethlehem to be killed. (Matthew 2:16.) The second is Herod Antipas, Tetrarch of Galilee and Perea from 4 B.C. to A.D. 39. He was the son of Herod the Great by a Samaritan wife named Malthace. Since his father was a native of Edom, Herod Antipas was a Jewish prince whose racial background was a blending of the blood of Samaria and Edom. He is the Herod before whom Jesus was tried. In Acts 12 we read of a Herod who kills James and arrests Peter. He is Herod Agrippa I, known as Herod the King. He was a grandson of Herod the Great, but not a son of Herod Antipas. Paul was tried before Herod Agrippa II, a son of Herod the King.

Jesus was probably referring to the Herods in general but particularly to Herod Antipas when He said to His disciples: "Take heed, beware of the leaven of the Pharisees, and of the leaven of Herod." (Mark 8:15.) In another setting, He also warns His disciples of the leaven of the Sadducees. (Matthew 16:6-12.) The leaven of the Pharisees was hypocrisy, the effort to present the show of religion without renewing the heart. The leaven of the Sadducees was unbelief. They did not believe in the resurrection from the dead or in angels or demons. The leaven of Herod was close to the leaven of the Sadducees. It was essentially the spirit of worldliness. In name, the Herods were Jewish princes. They paid lip service to the Jewish faith, but they lived for pleasure and power.

Herod's unwillingness to show any respect for the moral order was illustrated in his marriage to Herodias. She was a daughter of his half brother, Aristobulus, and the wife of another brother known as Herod Philip. Herod Antipas indulged a guilty passion for her while he was visiting his brother, Herod Philip, in Rome. Herod Antipas was at the time married to a daughter of Aretas, King of Arabia, but he sent her back to her father and married his brother's wife. The whole affair was typical of the license of the Herods. It outraged the Jewish conscience.

Herod came into contact with John the Baptist. Mark writes: "Herod feared John, knowing that he was a just man and an holy, and observed him; and when he heard him, he did many things, and heard him gladly." (Mark 6:20.) The meeting of Herod the Tetrarch with John the prophet might have had far-reaching consequences in the life of Herod. John was different from the other men Herod had known. The ruler respected the prophet for his courage and his influence with the people, and for a time listened to him and began to mend his ways.

But John laid his finger relentlessly on the sore spot of Herod's life. He said to him: "It is not lawful for thee to have thy brother's wife." (Mark 6:18.) We must admire John's courage in denouncing the sin of the monarch. It would have been expedient for John to have kept quiet. He could then have enjoyed the favor and protection of the ruler. But John knew that any genuine reformation in Herod's life would have to begin with the repudiation of his adulterous relation with Herodias. John paid a price for his fearlessness. He earned the undying hatred of an evil and powerful woman, and under her prodding Herod added to his other crimes the sin of shutting John up in prison. It was bad to flout the moral law and live in defiance of the word of the Lord, but it was worse to silence the voice of the Lord's messenger.

The story of Herod's execution of John is too familiar to need recounting in detail. Herod did not intend to do this. He was maneuvered into it by Herodias and Salome, her daughter by her former husband. But regardless of his motives, Herod cannot be relieved of the responsibility of having ordered the execution of the last and greatest of the prophets. In doing this he seared his conscience and brought to an abrupt end any tendency toward repentance and reform that might have existed in his life.

But Herod's conscience was not completely dead. Stories reached him of the appearance in Galilee of a greater prophet than John the Baptist. John had not performed any miracles, but this Prophet was mighty both in word and *deed*. Herod joined his contemporaries in the attempt to explain the miracles which God wrought through Jesus. Both Herod and Nicodemus faced works of power that could not easily be accounted for. Nicodemus was convinced by the miracles of Jesus that He was a teacher sent from God. Herod insisted that Jesus was John the Baptist risen from the dead. (Matthew 14:2.) Here we have the workings of a violated conscience. Herod was not certain that the argument between him and John the Baptist was ended when he gave the order to the executioner.

While Herod often heard of Jesus, he did not see Him until the day of His trial. Pilate was anxious to avoid the necessity of making a decision concerning Jesus. When he understood that Jesus was of Galilee he sent Him to Herod, who happened to be in Jerusalem at the time. We are given no indication of the emotions of Jesus as He stood in the presence of the man who had ordered John's death. We do know that Herod was glad to see Jesus. He hoped that Jesus would perform some miracle for him. We see the moral deterioriation of Herod in the fact that he faces Jesus with only the idle curiosity of one who hopes that Jesus will perform some tricks for the entertainment of him and his soldiers. He had heard John gladly. He stands now in the presence of a greater than John but he brings no sense of the need of forgiveness for his many crimes, culminating in the murder of John. He brings to Jesus nothing but the desire to see a miracle. And to him Jesus has nothing to say. Jesus could not speak the word of forgiveness because there was no repentance. He could have spoken a word of judgment, but the ruler who had not heard John was not likely to listen to Jesus. The most devastating comment we can make on the moral condition of Herod is to say that here was a man to whom Jesus had nothing to say.

There is, however, a word of Jesus to Herod. It was spoken while Jesus was in Perea on His way to Jerusalem. It probably came just a few weeks before their actual meeting. Some of the Pharisees came to Jesus, saying, "Get thee out, and depart hence: for Herod will kill thee." (Luke 13:31.) We do not know the motives of the Pharisees in bringing this message, and we do not know just how accurately they described Herod's intentions. We do know the answer of Jesus. He said to them: "Go ye, and tell that fox, Behold, I cast out devils, and I do cures to day and to morrow, and the third day I shall be perfected. Nevertheless I must walk to day, and to morrow, and the day following: for it cannot be that a prophet perish out of Jerusalem." (Luke 13:32-33.) Jesus calls Herod a fox. The fox is characterized by low cunning but not by courage. Jesus shows no fear of Herod. He intends to continue His work until He has finished and then to move on to Jerusalem. Herod's intentions will not affect His movements. We think here of that prayer of the disciples in Acts: "The kings of the earth stood up, and the rulers were gathered together against the Lord, and against his Christ. For of a truth against thy holy child Jesus, whom thou hast anointed, both *Herod*, and Pontius Pilate, with the Gentiles, and the people of Israel, were gathered together, for to do whatsoever thy hand and thy counsel determined before to be done." (Acts 4:26-28.)

The full irony of Jesus' words is expressed in that terrible statement: "It cannot be that a prophet perish out of Jerusalem." Of course the statement is not literally accurate. Prophets have perished outside of Jerusalem, and the Herods did kill prophets. We have only to remember John the Baptist and James the apostle for confirmation of this statement. But the Herods were not serious in their persecution of the prophets. Herod didn't intend to execute John, and Herod the King killed James with the sword to please the Jews. Compare their attitude with that of Saul of Tarsus when he sought to render God service by blotting out the sect of the Nazarenes and you can realize that the great persecutors were profoundly religious men. The prophet finds his center of opposition not in the worldly courts of the Herods but in the centers of religious orthodoxy. It is in Jerusalem, in the religious center of Judaism, that the Christ is to perish.

> *"Whom will ye that I release unto you? Barabbas, or Jesus which is called Christ? . . . They said, Barabbas."*
> —Matthew 27:17, 21.

36. BARABBAS

Scripture background: Matthew 27:15-26; Mark 15: 6-15; Luke 23:13-25; John 18:39-40; Acts 3:12-26.

Barabbas was a robber. The robber and the thief both commit crimes against property. The thief seeks to steal by cunning or stealth. The robber resorts to violence. In both cases, the crimes against property may easily lead to crimes against persons. If the thief is caught, he may kill in the attempt to escape, and the robber who seeks to overpower his victim may become a murderer. Barabbas was both a robber and a murderer. He was also a leader of insurrection. Palestine was a conquered country, and the robber bands made some show of resistance to Rome. Barabbas may have been a Zealot. He probably was about ninety per cent outlaw and ten per cent patriot. As the leader of this kind of band of robbers he had attained notoriety. But he had been caught and sentenced to death. He was lying in chains in the Roman prison.

Jesus and Barabbas were both prisoners. Against Jesus as against Barabbas there was the charge of being a leader of insurrection. When the chief priests sought to frame a charge against Jesus that would have standing in Pilate's court they had to accuse him of being a Zealot. The charge was not true. Jesus had refused to be this kind of Messiah. But He was accused of stirring up the people and attempting to make Himself the King of the Jews.

Luke passes from the story of Barabbas to the account of the women who followed Jesus weeping. Jesus tells them not to weep for Him but for themselves and for their children. He then predicts a time of terror in which they will wish that they had never borne children. He concludes with the saying: "For if they do these things in a green tree, what shall be done in the dry?" (Luke 23:31.) Oscar Cullmann interprets this to mean: "If the Romans execute *me* as a Zealot, who am no Zealot and who have always warned against Zealotism, what will they do then to the true Zealots!"* If this interpretation is correct, these words of Jesus are a prediction of the cruelty and brutality with which the Romans will crush a Jewish revolt. His words were abundantly fulfilled when the Romans destroyed the Jewish state in A.D. 70.

Barabbas was a Zealot. Jesus was not one, but He was accused of being dangerous to Rome. Pilate thought he could use Barabbas to help avoid making a decision concerning Jesus.

It was an established custom for the governor to release a political prisoner at the time of the feast. This was a show of clemency which was supposed to add to the rejoicing connected with the Passover. Pilate felt that if he gave the people the choice between Jesus and Barabbas they would certainly choose Jesus. He had been popular with the masses, and the common people had heard Him gladly. He had helped many of them. Barabbas was a robber and a murderer. Who would want him set at liberty?

But Pilate misjudged the situation. Persuaded by the priests, the

* Oscar Cullmann, *The State in the New Testament*, p. 48. New York: Charles Scribner's Sons, 1956. By permission.

people asked for Barabbas. Pilate gave them a second chance when he said to them: "What shall I do then with Jesus which is called Christ?" If they had asked for His release, Pilate was probably prepared to make a second gesture of clemency and release Jesus also. But to his surprise the multitude cried out, "Let him be crucified."

Pilate tried again. He called for water and made a show of washing his hands as he said to the multitude: "I am innocent of the blood of this just person: see ye to it." The people answered: "His blood be on us, and on our children." Pilate released Barabbas and sentenced Jesus to be crucified.

As we follow this story we feel, of course, the guilt of the chief priests. They are the moving force in the effort to destroy Jesus. They have mixed motives. They have feared His growing power. They may have had a genuine fear that in the end He might start a Messianic revolt which would bring about the destruction of their nation. They have been shocked by the audacity of His claims and in their own council they have condemned Him to death for blasphemy.

We do not excuse Pilate. He reveals a guilty conscience as he claims to be innocent of the death of Jesus. He cannot escape the charge of having used the power of the governor to condemn to death by crucifixion an innocent man.

But our major concern is with the people. The people of Jerusalem had the opportunity to save Jesus. If they had asked for His release, they would have gotten it; but they rejected Him and asked that a murderer be granted to them in His stead. Why did they do this?

It is obvious, of course, that they were persuaded by their leaders. But people do not have to yield to persuasion. The child in school is responsible if he is persuaded to cheat or steal. He does not have to let himself be persuaded. The Jerusalem mob may have been moved by an experience of disappointment. The people had expected Jesus to be their kind of Messiah. They had welcomed Him in His triumphal entry. But He did not seem to fit their idea of a Deliverer. Peter suggests that the multitude acted in ignorance. They were, of course, ignorant of the full dimensions of their crime. But after all, they knew the character of Barabbas. He was a leader of sedition, a robber, and a murderer. Jesus was a prophet, a teacher, and a healer who had gone about doing good. And the multitude rejected Jesus and chose Barabbas.

There is in the decision something of the element of offense. Jesus was not always gentle-mannered, meek, and mild. Some people loved Him and others hated Him. In Muncacsy's famous painting, *Christ Before Pilate*, there is a big burly man who is looking at Jesus and shouting: "Crucify him, crucify him!" The artist has made his face a picture of hate and ungovernable rage. The hate is directed at Jesus. Some men hated Jesus with a hatred which Barabbas never called forth. To many, He was a man of offense.

The people had their chance. They were given the choice between Jesus and Barabbas, and they chose Barabbas. The blame for the death of Jesus is not to be placed entirely on the scribes and the Pharisees, the chief priests and the elders, Pilate and Herod. The people share in this guilt. The people of a nation are responsible for their decisions. The German people cannot fully escape the responsibility of having let Hitler come to power or of having executed his infamous commands. And if the political leadership of a democracy is of a low order the people need to remember that they elect their leaders. If they elect rabble-rousers and timeservers when they need statesmen, they are in some measure responsible for their decisions.

The Jerusalem mob made its decision. They rejected Jesus and asked instead for a murderer and a robber. A few months later Peter and John faced another Jerusalem mob. Between the two scenes there is the fact of the Resurrection. Peter says to them: "The God of Abraham, and of Isaac, and of Jacob, the God of our fathers, hath glorified his Son Jesus; whom ye delivered up, and denied him in the presence of Pilate, when he was determined to let him go. But ye denied the Holy One and the Just, and desired a murderer to be granted unto you; and killed the Prince of life, whom God hath raised from the dead; whereof we are witnesses." (Acts 3:13-15.)

In the perspective of the Resurrection, the guilt of the multitude is seen in its deepest dimensions. They have rejected Jesus and asked that a murderer be granted them in His stead. God has reversed their decision and placed His approval on Jesus by raising Him from the dead. God has made the Jesus whom they crucified both Lord and Christ. Peter invites the people to change their decision in the light of God's action. Their decision is not final. God is coming to them through Jesus with His offer of mercy and forgiveness. The call to repentance and conversion is issued as the guilt of the multitude is seen in the light of the Resurrection. Peter concludes his message with the statement: "Unto you first God, having raised up his Son Jesus, sent him to bless you, in turning away every one of you from his iniquities." It is just possible that Barabbas heard this message and received as Saviour and Lord the man who was sentenced when he was released.

This decision concerning Jesus is the decision which every man must make. In a moment of doubt we may feel inclined to agree with the chief priests in their decision that He was a blasphemer. But if we accept the witness of the apostles to the Resurrection we can hardly fail to reverse this decision and agree with Peter that God has made this same Jesus both Lord and Christ.

> *"And they compel one Simon a Cyrenian . . . to bear his cross."—Mark 15:21.*

37. SIMON OF CYRENE

Scripture background: Matthew 27:32; Mark 15:21; Luke 23:26; John 19:17; Hebrews 13:11-13.

Jesus was in Pilate's judgment hall when the sentence of crucifixion was pronounced. The crucifixion took place outside the city walls at a spot known as Golgotha. The man condemned to be crucified was required to carry his cross from the judgment hall to the place of execution. This was part of the brutality of a system in which the Romans sought to terrorize a population by inflicting death on the condemned in the most cruel manner possible. Jesus went forth bearing His cross. There was nothing romantic about the cross He actually carried. It was made of heavy timbers fully braced. Its weight must have been almost unbearable on the back of one who had been recently flogged.

At some point on the road between the judgment hall and Golgotha, the soldiers met a man named Simon, whom they compelled to bear the cross. It has often been said that Jesus fell beneath the cross and that because He was unable to go further the soldiers forced Simon to carry it for Him. In some cathedrals the scene in which Jesus falls is depicted as one of the stages on the road to the cross. The tradition which says that Jesus fell under the weight of the cross does not have any foundation in Scripture, but it is probably substantially true to the facts. The soldiers would not have forced another man to carry the cross if they had felt that Jesus was able to carry it for Himself.

Simon was from Cyrene, a city on the northern coast of Africa. Because he came from a city of Africa, it has often been said that Simon was a member of the Negro race. This is possible but not probable. We should remember that the deep-seated distinctions based on color which plague the world today were unknown to the ancient world. Whether Simon came from Cyprus or Cyrene would have been a matter of indifference to the disciples of Jesus. But the probability is that Simon was a Jew of the Dispersion who was on his way to Jerusalem to worship at the Passover. There were men from Cyrene in the audience which heard the first Christian sermon at Pentecost. (Acts 2:10.) Later, unknown disciples from Cyprus and Cyrene took the crucial step of preaching the Gospel to Greeks at Antioch. (Acts 11:20.) In both cases, these men of Cyrene were Jews. While Simon was probably a Jew, he was unquestionably from Africa. When we remember the extent to which the people of Africa have been the burden bearers of the world it is interesting to know that a man of Africa was compelled to bear the cross of Christ.

The soldiers were within their rights in forcing Simon to bear the cross for Jesus. The Roman soldier could draft a civilian to carry a load for him. Jesus had this custom of the Roman soldiers in mind when He said in the Sermon on the Mount: "Whosoever shall compel thee to go a mile, go with him twain." (Matthew 5:41.) Simon must have felt fierce resentment at finding himself rudely interrupted in his journey and forced to carry the cross of a condemned man.

The Gospel narrative does not tell us anything more about Simon, but it is probable that in the end he became a Christian. Mark wrote his Gospel at Rome, and when he mentions Simon of Cyrene he identifies him as the father of Alexander and Rufus. (Mark 15:21.) Evidently Alexander and Rufus, the sons of Simon of Cyrene, were known to the Christian community at Rome. When Paul writes his letter to the Romans he says: "Salute Rufus chosen in the Lord, and his mother and mine." (Romans 16:13.) The identification here is precarious, but it is possible that the mother of Rufus and wife of Simon of Cyrene was so well known to Paul that he could refer to her as his mother. In any event we are probably on safe ground in assuming that Simon and his family became Christians. If this is correct, the event which was at first a source of humiliation to him became in the end a source of great satisfaction. It was here that he first met Jesus of Nazareth whom he afterward came to acknowledge as Lord. He must have been known in the Christian community as the man who had carried the cross of Christ.

In the story of Simon of Cyrene we see in vivid fashion the reality of the sufferings of Jesus. We know that the power of God was released through Jesus in a series of mighty deeds. We know that on the night of the arrest He felt that He could pray to God and receive twelve legions of angels. (Matthew 26:53.) But we know also that the power of God was never used to shield Him from suffering or to destroy the reality of His manhood. There is no more vivid illustration of this than the fact that the soldiers had to find another man to carry His cross. Jesus had passed through the agony of Gethsemane, through the various trials, and through at least one scourging. The soldiers must have felt that His physical strength was not equal to the ordeal of carrying His cross any further. In the figure of the Christ collapsed beneath the weight of the cross, we have a terrible symbol of the awful reality of His sufferings on Calvary.

This story illustrates also the *offense* of the cross. Simon was probably on his way to worship as a devout Jew at Passover. As he made the journey from Cyrene to Jerusalem he may have heard of Jesus of Nazareth as a prophet mighty in word and deed. He may have shared the hope of many that the prophet would at this time reveal Himself as the Christ. Suppose Simon had asked someone to point out to him the man whom many thought to be the Christ. And suppose that in answer someone had pointed him to the man who lay prostrate beneath the cross. Would this not give in vivid form the offense of the cross? Simon would have reasoned that the inability of Jesus of Nazareth to save Himself was proof that He was not the Christ. This was, in fact, the reasoning of both the friends and the enemies of Jesus. The chief priests were sure that His failure to come down from the cross was the final answer to all His mighty claims. The disciples passed into that despair in which they could only say that they *had* hoped that Jesus would be the Saviour of Israel. The Jews had no place in their thinking for a suffering and dying Messiah; and the Gentiles ridiculed the idea that a crucified Jew could be the Son of God, the Saviour of the world.

Simon must have felt in its fullness the offense of the cross. We can be sure that the event which changed his whole understanding of the meaning of Jesus' sufferings was the Resurrection. The risen Lord told Cleopas and his friend that it was necessary for the Christ to suffer these things, and to enter into His glory. (Luke 24:26.) When the disciples saw the cross in the light of the glory of the Resurrection they saw the suffering of the Christ in a new light. The writer of the letter to the Hebrews points to Jesus "who for the joy that was set before him endured the cross, despising the shame." (Hebrews 12:2.) When the disciples saw the cross in the light of the Resurrection they knew that Jesus had passed through this experience of suffering and shame in order that He might become the Saviour of mankind. They knew also that the love of God was revealed in His willingness to let His Son suffer for man's sin. Paul could write: "He that spared not his own Son, but delivered him up for us all, how shall he not with him also freely give us all things?" (Romans 8:32.) And again: "God commendeth his love toward us, in that, while we were yet sinners, Christ died for us." (Romans 5:8.)

Simon carried the cross of Christ. That cross could be carried only once. But the cross has become the symbol of the readiness of the Christ to suffer and die for the sins of His people. Jesus was thinking of the necessity of His suffering when He said: "I have a baptism to be baptized with; and how am I straitened till it be accomplished." (Luke 12:50.) There is a sense in which we cannot share the sufferings of the Christ. There is a mystery and depth about His pain which we cannot fully understand, but in a limited fashion we can enter into the fellowship of His sufferings. He said to the sons of Zebedee: "Can ye drink of the cup that I drink of? and be baptized with the baptism that I am baptized with?" They said unto Him, "*We can.*" And He said to them: "Ye shall indeed drink of the cup that I drink of; and with the baptism that I am baptized withal shall ye be baptized." (Mark 10:38-39.) We can share with Jesus His compassion for lost men. We can enter into His love of righteousness and His hatred of iniquity. We can be ready to follow Him even if it means suffering and death. In fact, Jesus has said that the willingness to bear a cross in following Him is a condition of genuine discipleship. He has said: "Whosoever doth not bear his cross, and come after me, cannot be my disciple." (Luke 14:27.) We cannot bear the cross that Simon carried, but we must be ready to follow Jesus until we know the meaning of bearing the cross that is ours.

*"To day shalt thou be with me in paradise."—Luke
23:43.*

38. THE THIEF ON THE CROSS

*Scripture background: Isaiah 53:12; Matthew 27:38;
Mark 15:27-28; Luke 22:37; 23:32-43.*

Jesus was crucified between two thieves. He Himself
had said that in His fulfillment of the mission of the Suffering
Servant He must be "reckoned among the transgressors." (Luke
22:37; see also Isaiah 53:12.) The identification of Jesus with sinners was complete. He was sentenced to death as a criminal. *This*
prophecy concerning the Suffering Servant was fulfilled when
Jesus died on the cross. In its deeper meaning its fulfillment was
in no sense conditioned upon His actually being crucified between
two thieves, but the writers of the New Testament were right in
seeing in this event a symbol of the way in which Jesus was
numbered with the transgressors.

Jesus died between two thieves. The established social order
is endangered by those who fall below its standards and by those
who rise above them. The prophet and the criminal are dangerous in a different way, but they both call in question some of the
basic assumptions of the established order. The thief is guilty of
crimes against property. If he is not checked and punished, no
man will be secure in his possessions. The rulers of society know
what to do with thieves. They are not quite so sure of the best
way to handle prophets. They are more afraid of prophets than of
thieves. When the leaders of the Jews felt that Jesus was en-
dangering their whole way of life, they were ready to unite to
destroy Him.

The thieves who were crucified with Jesus were called male-
factors; that is, evildoers. They were bad men. Thieving always

involves deception. With the loss of respect for truth the whole character is undermined, and the thief is usually prepared to injure others in order to save himself. The severity of their punishment would lead us to conclude that the men who were crucified with Jesus were hardened criminals. In modern terms, they were gangsters who had finally been caught, convicted, and sentenced to death.

These thieves may not have known much about Jesus before they found themselves condemned to be crucified with Him. But they could not have failed to learn from the events connected with the crucifixion something of the charges against the man who was crucified between them. In the inscription over the cross, He was called the King of the Jews. And the enemies of Jesus spoke with scorn of His claim to be the Christ. The thieves joined in this mockery. One of them said to Him: "If thou be Christ, save thyself and us." (Luke 23:39.) This was spoken in derision. We do not defend the attitude of this man but we can see the basis of his ridicule. The person whom he saw seemingly helpless on the cross was far removed from the Jewish idea of the Christ. We see here the offense of the cross in its darkest terms.

But the man's companion in crime passed at this time through a remarkable change of attitude. He administered a stern rebuke to the other thief as he said: "Dost not thou fear God, seeing thou art in the same condemnation? And we indeed justly; for we receive the due reward of our deeds: but this man hath done nothing amiss." (Luke 23:40-41.) He begins with an appeal to the fear of God. The fear of the Lord is the beginning of wisdom. The fear of God involves the fear of violating the commands of God. Neither of these men had lived in the fear of the Lord. They had both broken the eighth commandment. But as this man faces the death which he knows now is not far away, he suddenly becomes aware of the moral order which he has violated. He is particularly conscious of this because he knows that both he and his companion have one thing in common with Jesus. All three are sentenced to death. God's judgment is not limited to the time of death. God as the vindicator of the

moral order has so ordered our world that men do not violate
His laws with impunity. But there is a peculiar sense in which
the time of death is the time of judgment. "It is appointed unto
men once to die, but after this the judgment." (Hebrews 9:27.)

In the light of this coming judgment, this man makes a re-
appraisal of his life. No man should wait for a deathbed repentance. Usually men die as they have lived. The time for every
man to repent is now. Someone has said that the Bible records
one deathbed repentance that no man may despair, and only one
that no man may presume.

As this man looks back over his past he sees the true nature of
his life of crime. He knows that he has broken God's commandments. He knows that sin deserves punishment. And in the midst
of the unspeakable torture of death by crucifixion, he acknowledges that his sentence is just. In this he knows that he stands in
sharp contrast to Jesus. He knows that Jesus is dying as an innocent man. He says of Him, "This man hath done nothing amiss."
He is certain that Jesus has done nothing to justify the terrible
sentence which He has received.

Up to this point his words have been directed to his companion
in crime. But he now turns to Jesus and says: "Jesus, remember
me when thou comest in thy kingdom." (Luke 23:42, A.S.V.) The
most amazing thing about this request is the faith in Jesus which
underlies it. This man is speaking to Jesus as He hangs on the
cross, but he penetrates the offense of the cross and dares to believe that Jesus will come into His Kingdom. And he believes
that Jesus, when He does come into His Kingdom, will be able to
help him. We do not know how this man came to this faith. He
may have been impressed by the majesty of Jesus' bearing in the
hour of His suffering. We do know that he sees beyond the cross
and believes that Jesus will come into His glory.

The words, "Jesus, remember me," are words which we, too,
can speak to Jesus in our hour of need as we stand in the presence
of death. We know that He is both our crucified and our risen
Lord. We know that He is seated in glory at the right hand of
God. For everyone there comes a time when he must go out

into the great unknown. In such a time the help of man is vain. In the hour of death we must look to Jesus and say, "Lord, remember me." He has gone to prepare a place for us. He has promised to come again and receive us unto Himself. (John 14:2-3.) And we must pray, "Lord, do not forget *me* in *my* time of need."

Jesus has ignored the taunts of His enemies but He does not fail to hear the cry of faith. He says to the dying thief: "To day shalt thou be with me in paradise." We cannot fail to be impressed by the confidence which Jesus has in His ultimate victory. He knows that His hour has come. He is passing through suffering and death, but He knows that this time is His hour of victory. He speaks the forgiveness of God in answer to the prayer of faith. We face the mystery of a forgiveness that covers a life of crime with the word of pardon. But it is not possible to say that the forgiveness of God is cheap when that forgiveness is based on an atonement in which the Son of God dies for the sin of man.

The words of Jesus to the dying thief contain the promise of His presence. "Thou shalt be with me." This is the heart of the Christian's hope of eternal life. When Jesus says, "To day," He gives more than the man has asked. The man has pleaded to be remembered when Jesus comes into His Kingdom. Jesus promises that he shall pass immediately into Paradise. We do not need to define the precise meaning of Paradise in this sentence. It points to the resurrection world of God which lies beyond time and space. It contrasts strangely with the world of suffering, sin, and hate in which the repentant thief draws near to death. This word of Jesus suggests the sentence from the Shorter Catechism which says: "The souls of believers are at their death made perfect in holiness, and do immediately pass into glory."*

Jesus gives the repentant thief an infinitely greater deliverance than that which had been asked in mockery by his companion, who had said: "Save thyself and us." (Luke 23:39.) And the story of the thieves reminds us of the decisive nature of the element of personal response. Two thieves were crucified with

* The Westminster Shorter Catechism, Question 37.

Jesus. One of them went out into eternity having added to his other sins the crime of mocking the Son of God in His dying hour. The other looked to Jesus in faith and received from Him the promise of an immediate entrance into an eternal salvation. It is to those who receive Him that Jesus gives the power to become sons of God. (John 1:12.)

"Truly this man was the Son of God."—Mark 15:39.

39. THE CENTURION AT THE CROSS

Scripture background: Matthew 27:24-31, 50-54; Mark 15:16-20, 37-39, 43-45; Luke 23:46-47; John 19:23-24, 31-37.

When Pilate sentenced Jesus to death by crucifixion, he committed to a Roman centurion the responsibility of carrying out the details of the order of execution. Oscar Cullmann is probably right in saying that Jesus was crucified as a Zealot.* He was put to death by the Romans because He was accused of claiming to be the king of the Jews. When the death sentence is given today, the state seeks to bring death as quickly and as painlessly as possible. But the Romans operated on the theory that death by torture would be more effective as a deterrent from crime than death in some easier way. The Roman soldiers who had retained any moral sensibilities must have detested the assignment of serving as executioners for Pilate, but they had to obey the orders they received.

It is probable that this Roman centurion had in the beginning formed no clearly fixed opinions concerning Jesus of Nazareth. As the day went on he must have come increasingly to the conviction that Roman justice had miscarried in the crucifixion of this man. He was placed in the position of having to put to

* Oscar Cullmann, *The State in the New Testament*, p. 22.

death by torture a man whom he was convinced was innocent. The dilemma of the Roman centurion raises the whole question of the moral involvement of those who must act under orders. The basic guilt for Jesus' death rested with the religious leaders of the Jews. The chief priests, the scribes and Pharisees, and the Herodians were united in the decision that Jesus must be destroyed. Pilate and Herod shared in this guilt. Pilate in particular ordered the death by crucifixion of a man whom he knew was not guilty. But there is some moral responsibility on the part of the men who actually crucified Jesus. A similar moral dilemma was faced by the soldier who dropped the first atomic bomb. Soldiers have been known to refuse to carry out orders which were revolting to them.

Even if we excuse the centurion from any moral guilt in carrying out orders he dared not disobey, we cannot excuse him for permitting his soldiers to mock the prisoner. To the Romans the charge that Jesus was a king of the Jews seemed to lend itself to ridicule. The Prophet from Nazareth did not fit into the Roman conception of a king. It was the Roman soldiers who gave Jesus the crown of thorns, clothed Him with a purple robe, the symbol of royalty, and placed a scepter in His hands. The centurion should never have allowed his men to behave in such a manner.

But he who had permitted his men to engage in mockery came in time to have a profound respect for the man he was crucifying. We do not know the process which brought about the centurion's change in attitude. He may have observed the majesty with which Jesus bore the ridicule of the soldiers. As he watched the crucifixion, he must have seen the compassion of Jesus as He committed His mother to the beloved disciple. He may have heard Jesus' words to the thief on the cross. He could not avoid listening to the taunts of His enemies, and he must have heard the prayer of Jesus when He said: "Father, forgive them; for they know not what they do." (Luke 23:34.) We know that the centurion was so impressed by what he had seen and heard at the death of Jesus that he said: "Certainly this was a righteous man." (Luke 23:47.)

The centurion's conclusion will be affirmed by all who examine closely the words and deeds of Jesus of Nazareth. When we see this man we must feel that He is a righteous man. Follow Jesus in His ministry of healing. See Him in His compassion for the multitude as they faint and are scattered abroad. See Him in His love for His disciples. Listen to Him in His condemnation of the scribes and Pharisees. Feel His hatred of hypocrisy and graft. If we have the capacity to know the difference between good and evil, we must know that Jesus is good. If we can distinguish between hate and love, we must be sure that Jesus is a man of love. The centurion was right. This was a *righteous* man.

The centurion came to a deeper appreciation of Jesus. There was always about Jesus an overtone of something that was more than human, and the events connected with the crucifixion were calculated to bring to the centurion a sense of wonder and awe. He could not have failed to notice the supernatural darkness. The cause of this we do not know, but even an unexpected eclipse of the sun can bring about a feeling of dread. We experience with awe the wonder of darkness in the middle of the day.

The centurion cannot have failed to hear the mockery that was based on the claim that Jesus was the Son of God. Those who reviled Jesus said to Him: "If thou be the Son of God, come down from the cross." (Matthew 27:40.) The chief priests said: "He trusted in God; let him deliver him now, if he will have him: for he said, I am the Son of God." (Matthew 27:43.) The centurion must have wondered if by any chance the enemies of Jesus could be mistaken. He must have asked himself if it could be possible for the man he was crucifying to be the Son of God. The centurion witnessed the death of Jesus. He must have heard the words Jesus spoke as the end drew near. He was there when Jesus in the midst of the inexplicable darkness called out in Aramaic: "Eli, Eli, lama sabachthani?" The words are translated: "My God, my God, why hast thou forsaken me?" (Matthew 27:46.) The centurion could not have understood the full import of these words, but he must have sensed the tremendous spiritual struggle they revealed. He must have heard the words, "It is finished." (John 19:30.) He was there when Jesus cried with a loud voice, "Father, into thy hands I commend my spirit." The words of the dying Christ profoundly affected the centurion as he stood near the cross. Could it be that the man who cried out in those words was indeed the Son of God?

The centurion watched as the Christ died. The King James Version says simply that "he gave up the ghost." The words do not carry for us the meaning that they had in Elizabethan English. The word "ghost" meant a disembodied spirit. The Revised Standard Version translates it "he breathed his last." This is true, but it is not exhaustive. When the body ceases to breathe we know that life is gone, but the deeper truth is that the *spirit* leaves the body. We can only know embodied spirit. But we feel that the inner core of the personality is not in the body. The centurion watched as the spirit which had animated the body of Jesus in the days of His flesh departed. He heard the words of Jesus as He yielded up His spirit with a strong cry to the keeping of His Father. It has been said that Socrates died like a man but Jesus Christ died like a god. The centurion who stood beside the cross and watched Jesus die did not need the added terror of the earthquake to be convinced that this man was more than human.

We must not think that the centurion passed at once to fullness of faith in Jesus Christ as the Son of God. He was a Roman, and the doors of the Church were not opened to Gentiles until some years later. But the centurion does express a conviction which comes to those who meditate deeply on the meaning of the death of Christ. When we see Him in His passion and death we are certain to feel that there is more involved than the death of a righteous man.

When Joseph of Arimathaea asks for the body of Jesus, Pilate is amazed to learn that He is already dead. He does not deliver the body to Joseph until he has sent for the centurion and received from him the statement that Jesus is indeed dead. (Mark 15:44-45.) In the scene that follows between Pilate and the chief priests, we have the feeling that neither Pilate nor the chief priests are quite sure that their victory over Jesus of Nazareth is complete when His body has been placed in Joseph's tomb. There may be a touch of irony in Pilate's words as he says to the chief priests: "Ye have a watch: go your way, make it as sure as ye can." (Matthew 27:65.)

The Scriptures drop the curtain of silence on this Roman centurion as he certifies to Pilate that Jesus is dead. But he cannot have failed to hear the rumors concerning the empty tomb and the appearance of the risen Lord. We can at least hope that the centurion who crucified Jesus came in time to acknowledge as his Saviour and Lord the man he had crucified. The Scriptures do not leave us with a dead Christ. They pass from the witness of the centurion to Pilate to the witness of the apostles to the empty grave and the risen Lord. They are written that we may come with Thomas to the acknowledgment of Jesus as our Lord and our God.

"A disciple of Jesus, but secretly for fear of the Jews."
—John 19:38.

40 JOSEPH OF ARIMATHAEA

Scripture background: Matthew 27:57-60; Mark 15: 43-45; Luke 23:50-56; John 19:38-42.

Joseph came from Arimathaea, identified by John as a city of the Jews. The word Arimathaea is a Greek translation of the Aramaic word Ramah. We cannot say just where this city was located, but the Joseph who gave burial to the body of Jesus is always referred to as "of Arimathaea" to distinguish him from the other Josephs of Scripture.

We are told that Joseph was a good man and a just. These are words of high praise. They describe a man of proved integrity who was consistently fair in his dealings with others. Mark tells us that Joseph was a respected member of the council. This probably means that he was a member of the Sanhedrin. While Joseph was originally from Arimathaea, he must have lived in Jerusalem long enough to be established as one of the city's most respected citizens.

Joseph is described as one who "waited for the kingdom of God." (Mark 15:43.) He shared the hopes of his people for the coming of the Kingdom of God. Joseph was a rich man. We do not know the extent of his wealth, but the suggestion is that he was outstanding both for his character and for his wealth. Jesus did not have many contacts with rich people. Two of His followers, Matthew and Zacchaeus, may have been men of some wealth, but they were publicans who had riches without honor. The rich young ruler came to Jesus but went away sorrowful because he had great possessions. Joseph was probably the richest man among the early followers of Jesus.

The suggestions of the story are that Joseph was not a young man. He owned property near Jerusalem but outside the city walls. He had here a garden and in this garden he had prepared his own tomb. It was hewn out of the rock, and no one had ever been buried there. Joseph was old and rich and respectable. He had prepared his tomb and he was waiting for the Kingdom of God.

Joseph was a man who believed in Jesus. As he was waiting for the Kingdom of God, he must have heard with great interest of the appearance of a Prophet from Nazareth who announced that the Kingdom of God had come and called men to repentance. Joseph must have observed the mighty works of Jesus. He may have been among those who, with Nicodemus, reached the conclusion that Jesus must be a teacher sent from God since no one could do the works He was doing if God was not with Him. Joseph probably heard Jesus teach and preach. He may have shared the feeling of the soldiers who said, "Never man spake like this man." (John 7:46.) We do not know the details of the contacts which Joseph had with Jesus, but we do know that he reached in his heart the conviction that Jesus was indeed the Christ, the Saviour of His people.

But Joseph was a secret disciple. He kept his convictions to himself. He had never publicly acknowledged his faith in Jesus. He was a disciple of Jesus but secretly *for fear of the Jews*. In the circles in which Joseph moved it was not popular to acknowledge faith in Jesus. The members of the council reminded Nicodemus that none of the Pharisees or the rulers had believed on Jesus. They insisted that His followers were drawn exclusively from the multitude that knew not the law. (John 7:48-49.) But Joseph of Arimathaea was not alone among the rulers in his convictions concerning Jesus. John writes: "Nevertheless among the chief rulers also many believed on him; but because of the Pharisees they did not confess him, lest they should be put out of the synagogue: for they loved the praise of men more than the praise of God." (John 12:42-43.) Joseph's wealth may have had something to do with his caution. When men have great possessions they have much to lose. They have a large stake in the *status quo*. We do not know all the causes of his indecision, but we do know that Joseph of Arimathaea did not openly confess his faith.

Jesus demands public confession. We can be sure of His sympathy with those who are moving through doubt to faith. He dealt in this manner with the doubts of Thomas. But Jesus spoke plainly on the subject of secret discipleship. He said: "Whosoever therefore shall confess me before men, him will I confess also before my Father which is in heaven. But whosoever shall deny me before men, him will I also deny before my Father which is in heaven." (Matthew 10:32-33.) This is the unity of faith and baptism. Faith involves the inner movement of the heart in response to the love of God in Christ. Baptism is the rite of initiation into the fellowship of the people of God. Baptism without faith is hypocrisy, but faith which does not lead to confession points to a surrender which is not yet complete. If Joseph of Arimathaea while he was still a secret disciple had been called to pass through death to the judgment bar of God, he would not have met the full conditions of discipleship. We must remember the words of Jesus: "Whosoever shall deny me before men, him will I also deny before my Father which is in heaven."

Joseph found the role of secret discipleship increasingly intolerable. He was a member of the Sanhedrin, but he did not agree with the policies of this body with regard to Jesus. Under the leadership of Caiaphas, the council reached the decision that Jesus must be destroyed. Joseph did not agree with this purpose of the council, but he did nothing openly to oppose it. He lived to see the plan of the council translated into action. He may have sat with the court which found Jesus guilty of blasphemy and sentenced Him to death. If he was there, he obviously felt that this was a time for the prudent to keep silence. But it is difficult to imagine the inner conflict in the soul of Joseph. He found himself in this way a partner to the decision in which One whom in his heart he believed to be the Christ was condemned to death. Joseph faced in an acute form the dilemma which is always with the secret disciple. He believes one way and is forced to act another. The inner tension in the heart of Joseph must have reached the breaking point when Jesus was crucified on a hill called Calvary which was close to the garden in which Joseph had prepared his own tomb.

Joseph did nothing until he knew that Jesus was dead, but at last courage took the place of fear. He walked *boldly* into the hall of Pilate and asked of him the body of Jesus. This act was both an expression of his desire to give burial to the body and an acknowledgment to Pilate and the Jews that he was a disciple of Jesus. Pilate was amazed to find that Jesus was dead. He kept Joseph waiting until he had sent for the centurion and confirmed Joseph's statement concerning the death of Jesus. When all doubt about the death of Jesus had been removed, Pilate granted the body to Joseph. And as Joseph went from the hall of Pilate to claim the body of Jesus he reaped the first fruit of his decision. His friend Nicodemus joined him and went with him to Calvary. God had used the decision of Joseph to bring Nicodemus also to the place of decision. The rich man and the scholar walked together to the cross.

Joseph of Arimathaea will always be remembered as the man who gave decent burial to the body of Jesus. Without the action of Joseph, the body of Jesus would have been thrown unburied on the place of refuse, along with the bodies of the two thieves. In the providence of God, Joseph prepared the way for the centurion's report concerning the death of Jesus, for the burial of the body in his own new tomb, for the rolling of the great stone to close the sepulcher, for the request of the chief priests for a watch at the tomb, and for Pilate's order granting the watch and sealing the tomb.

The action of Joseph prepared the way also for the witness to the empty tomb. The Christian faith rests on more than an empty tomb. The disciples were transformed from disappointment and sorrow to great joy by the appearance to them of the risen Lord. Jesus showed Himself alive to them after His passion "by many infallible proofs, being seen of them forty days, and speaking of the things pertaining to the kingdom of God." (Acts 1:3.) In their witness to the Resurrection, the disciples of Jesus pointed to an event which happened at a definite time and place. Jesus rose on Sunday morning after the Passover in the year A.D. 30. This event took place in Palestine in the tomb of Joseph of Arimathaea. Joseph found himself the owner of the most significant spot on earth, the place at which "God . . . brought again from the dead our Lord Jesus, that great shepherd of the sheep, through the blood of the everlasting covenant." (Hebrews 13:20.)

The apostles bore witness to an event which came at a definite time and place. But the meaning of this event affects every human being. Paul gives the significance of the Resurrection as he writes: "The word of faith, which we preach; that if thou shalt confess with thy mouth the Lord Jesus, and shalt believe in thine heart that God hath raised him from the dead, thou shalt be saved." (Romans 10:8-9.) Here we have again the unity of inward faith and outward confession and the impossibility of secret discipleship.

"Mary Magdalene came and told the disciples that she had seen the Lord."—John 20:18.

41. MARY MAGDALENE

Scripture background: Matthew 27:56-61; 28:1-10; Mark 15:40-47; 16:1-11; Luke 8:1-3; 24:1-12; John 20:1-18.

Mary Magdalene was the leader of the women who were the first to discover the empty tomb. She was the first person to whom the risen Lord "shewed himself alive after his passion." (Acts 1:3.)

She was called Mary Magdalene. The name Magdalene probably comes from Magdala, a small village west of the Sea of Galilee. Mary has always been a popular name for women. Among the women who are mentioned in the Gospels we have Mary the mother of Jesus; Mary of Bethany, the sister of Lazarus; Mary the mother of James and Joseph; Mary the wife of Cleopas; Mary the mother of John Mark; possibly another woman known as the other Mary; and Mary Magdalene. In such a company of women named Mary it was necessary to use a second name to distinguish personalities. For this reason the Mary who came from Magdala is always known as Mary Magdalene.

In his first reference to her, Luke speaks of certain women, "which had been healed of evil spirits and infirmities." He then mentions specifically "Mary called Magdalene, out of whom went seven devils." (Luke 8:2.) And Mark writes: "Now when Jesus was risen early the first day of the week, he appeared first to Mary Magdalene, out of whom he had cast seven devils." (Mark 16:9.) There are various ways of interpreting the casting out of the seven devils. Mary Magdalene has been thought of as a fallen woman, a sinner, whom Jesus restored to purity. In fact, the word *magdalen* has been used to describe the reformed prostitute. This is one of the definitions given to the word in the dictionary. (Webster's New Collegiate.) But there is no basis whatever in Scripture for this interpretation of the past of Mary Magdalene. She is first mentioned in Luke in the beginning of chapter 8. The reference to her follows immediately after the story of the unknown woman who came to Jesus in the home of Simon the leper, but we have no reason to identify this woman with either Mary Magdalene or Mary of Bethany. Jesus received into the Kingdom of God publicans and harlots. When He forgave their past He blotted out its power to come between the sinners and Himself. But we have no reason to cast doubt on the purity of Mary Magdalene.

Another popular interpretation has been to identify the seven devils which were cast out of Mary Magdalene with the seven deadly sins. This interpretation was pictured in dramatic form in the picture, *The King of Kings*. The seven deadly sins are usually listed as pride, envy, wrath, sloth, covetousness, gluttony, and lust. The most effective way to find victory over these and similar sins is through the surrender of life to Jesus Christ. When He is acknowledged as Lord, the house of our life is no longer swept and garnished but left without an occupant. Jesus came to save us from our sins—even the seven deadly sins—but there is no reason to think that this is a correct interpretation of the experience of Mary of Magdala.

We are closer to the truth when we think of devil possession as a condition which affected the core of Mary's personality. She may have been under the power of evil spirits, or she may have had a disease similar to some of the diseases today which are usually called insanity. In either case, the affliction struck at the center of her personality and left her in pitiable condition. Jesus found her as she was disintegrating in her inner life, and He restored her to sanity and health. It is interesting to notice that Mary Magdalene is the only one of the personalities around Jesus known to us by name who was healed by Him. The case of Lazarus would fall into a somewhat different category. Jesus did not come to him while he was sick. But He did restore him to life after he had been dead four days.

Mary Magdalene gave to Jesus as her Saviour the full devotion of her woman's heart. Luke tells us that she ministered unto Him of her substance. Her love expressed itself in the giving of her possessions to the needs of Jesus and His apostles. In this she did not work alone. We would not be far wrong if we said that she was part of the first Ladies' Aid Society. She worked with a group of like-minded women of whom Luke mentions Joanna, the wife of Herod's steward Chuza, and Susanna. We read in John 12:6 of the common purse which Judas carried, and we learn that it was the custom for gifts to be made from it to the poor. (John 13:29.) We can be sure that this purse was supplied in part by Mary and the women associated with her.

Mary became the leader of a band of women who at times followed Jesus in His preaching missions in Galilee. Luke writes: "And it came to pass afterward, that he went throughout every city and village, preaching and shewing the glad tidings of the kingdom of God: *and the twelve were with him, and certain women.*" Mary Magdalene is always named first among these women. Who can measure the loving ministry which Mary Magdalene and the women who worked with her must have performed to our Lord and His disciples as they journeyed through Galilee?

Mary Magdalene was present at the crucifixion. Here also she appears as the leader of many women who have followed Jesus from Galilee, ministering unto Him. (Matthew 27:55.) At first these women stand on the fringes of the crowd beholding the crucifixion from afar. Later we find that Mary Magdalene and Mary the wife of Cleopas are with Mary the mother of Jesus at the foot of the cross. We know that Mary Magdalene and some of the women who were with her stayed through the earthquake and the supernatural darkness. They were present when Jesus died. They were still there when Joseph of Arimathaea and Nicodemus came with the permission of Pilate to remove the body. They followed these men as they bore the body of Jesus from

Calvary's hill to Joseph's garden. They watched when the stone was placed at the mouth of the sepulcher. (Mark 15:47.) And when Joseph went away he left Mary Magdalene and the other Mary sitting there. A little later she returned to the place of lodging to rest on the Sabbath day according to the commandment. (Luke 23:56.)

We can only surmise the emotions of Mary as she rested on that Sabbath day. She knew, of course, a crushing sense of personal loss. The one to whom she had given the deepest devotion of her life had been brutally killed before her eyes. But personal loss was merged with despair for her country. She must have shared with Cleopas the hopelessness which is expressed in the words: "We trusted that it had been he which should have redeemed Israel." (Luke 24:21.)

The women rested the seventh day. These women of Galilee shame us in their observance of the fourth commandment. But long before dawn on Sunday, Mary Magdalene and the women who followed her were on their way to the sepulcher. They intended to pay the last tribute of love in the anointing of the body of Jesus. We do not have the information necessary to bring all the accounts of the Resurrection into complete harmony, but the narratives are in agreement concerning the empty tomb and the appearance of the risen Lord. In the presence of such a stupendous event some differences in detail are to be expected. We will follow the story as John tells it. It would seem that Mary was leading the women as they came to the tomb. Probably she was the first to see that the stone was removed. She must have hastened at once to take this news to Peter and John. She does not come to them as the bearer of good news. She says: "They have taken away the Lord out of the sepulchre, and we know not where they have laid him." (John 20:2.) We do not need to follow here the story of Peter and John as they run to the sepulcher.

After the two apostles leave, Mary remains at the tomb and observes "two angels in white sitting, the one at the head, and the other at the feet, where the body of Jesus had lain." They say to her: "Woman, why weepest thou?" She replies: "Because they have taken away my Lord, and I know not where they have laid him." Even the vision of angels does not bring hope to the heart of Mary. This indicates the depth of her sorrow and despair.

The risen Lord comes to her in her grief. He repeats the words of the angels, "Woman, why weepest thou?" But He adds the question, "Whom seekest thou?" These are the first recorded words of the risen Lord. Mary assumes that the speaker is the gardener. She assumes also that he knows of the One she seeks. She places no limits on her woman's strength as she asks for permission to carry away the body of her Lord. Jesus calls her name. He must have spoken it even as she had heard Him call her many times on the roads of Galilee. As she hears her name she knows Him and answers with the term by which she had been accustomed to address Him, "Rabboni."

Jesus says to Mary: "Touch me not; for I am not yet ascended to my Father: but go to my brethren, and say unto them, I ascend unto my Father, and your Father; and to my God, and your God." (John 20:17.) Westcott says that we should interpret the words "Touch me not" as meaning "Do not cling to me."* Probably Mary has thrown herself at His feet and is holding to Him. She has not fully understood the nature of the resurrection she has witnessed. She is thinking that her Lord has returned to the former life even as life came again to the body of Lazarus. But she is witnessing the Resurrection, not a resuscitation. She is in the presence of One who comes as the first-born from the dead. She is seeing on earth that which bears witness to the resurrection life of God. There will not be a return to the days of His flesh when she followed Him through Galilee. But the risen Lord who is ascending to His Father will give to her and to all who believe on Him the promise of His presence. Mary is to bear to the disciples the words of the risen Lord who will be forever with His people.

* Brooke Foss Westcott, *The Gospel According to St. John*, pp. 344-345. Grand Rapids: Wm. B. Eerdmans, 1954.

*"Was it not necessary that the Christ should suffer
these things and enter into his glory?—Luke 24:26, R.S.V.*

42. CLEOPAS

Scripture background: Luke 24:13-47.

Cleopas and his friend were walking the road to Emmaus. It was late afternoon of the Sunday following the crucifixion of Jesus on Friday. As the men walked, they talked, and their conversation centered on the events that had recently taken place in Jerusalem.

Both of them were followers of Jesus of Nazareth. They had recognized in Him "a prophet mighty in deed and word before God and all the people." They had heard Jesus teach, and His words had come to them with a note of authority. They were sure that He was the bearer of the word of the Lord. They had seen His mighty deeds and, like Nicodemus, they had been convinced that no man could do the things that Jesus did unless God was with Him. Because they believed Jesus to be a true prophet they had become His followers.

These men had carried in their hearts a great hope. They had believed that Jesus was "the one to redeem Israel." (Luke 24:21, R.S.V.) We do not know the full content of their hope, but probably they thought Jesus would deliver the people of Israel from their bondage to Rome. Their hope must have gone deeper than the desire for political deliverance. They were waiting for a king who would establish again the throne of David and give to Israel a reign of righteousness and peace. They had believed that Jesus of Nazareth was the Lord's Anointed. They were confident that He was a man sent from God for the deliverance of His people, Israel.

Now the hope which had recently burned so brightly was dead, crushed by the events of the weekend. Cleopas saw the chief priests and the leaders of his people deliver Jesus to the

Romans to be crucified. He may have been present at the crucifixion. Perhaps he carried in his heart the hope that Jesus would
come down from the cross to silence His enemies and proclaim
Himself the Christ. But Jesus had not come down. As he walked
the road to Emmaus, Cleopas believed that the Jesus in whom he
had placed his hope was crucified, dead, and buried.

The death of Jesus was to Cleopas proof that his confidence
had been misplaced. He had no place in his thinking for a suffering and dying Messiah. The hope which had given meaning to
his life turned to dull despair. There was, however, one discon-
certing note in the picture. Certain women had gone to the tomb
early that morning and had found the tomb empty. Cleopas had
heard their report of a vision of angels who said that Jesus was
alive. He knew, too, that the story of the empty tomb had been
confirmed by a visit of Peter and John to the sepulcher. But
these stories, not easily explained, had not come to Cleopas as
a word of hope. He knew that the tomb was empty, but he had
not come to believe in the reality of the risen Lord.

As Cleopas and his friend walked and talked together, a
Stranger joined them on the road to Emmaus. He entered into
conversation with them, and in response to His questions they
told the story of their hope and disappointment. When they had
finished, the Stranger said to them: "O foolish men, and slow of
heart to believe all that the prophets have spoken! Was it not
necessary that the Christ should suffer these things and enter
into his glory?" (Luke 24:25-26, R.S.V.) In the first sentence we
have the concern of the teacher who sees the full truth and
marvels at the slowness with which others lay hold of it. The
heart of His message to Cleopas is in the question: "Was it not
necessary that the Christ should suffer these things and enter into
his glory?" Jesus speaks in the form of a question, but through
it He is saying to Cleopas: "It was necessary for the Christ to
suffer these things and to enter into his glory." It is here that He
speaks to the need of Cleopas. Cleopas cannot believe that Jesus
is the Christ because to him the suffering and death of Jesus are
a contradiction of His claim to be the Christ. But the Stranger

tells Cleopas that it was necessary for the Christ to suffer these things if He was to enter into His glory.

As they walk together the Stranger opens to Cleopas the meaning of the sacred writings of his people. We cannot reconstruct His message, but we can be sure that Jesus made reference to the figure of the Suffering Servant in the fifty-third chapter of Isaiah. Here the Servant of the Lord becomes the sin-bearer who through His vicarious suffering atones for the sin of His people. He may have shown the way in which the sacrificial system pointed beyond itself to the great sacrifice that had to be made.

It is clear also that Jesus in the days of His flesh moved toward the cross with a sense of inner necessity. When at Caesarea Philippi He acknowledges Himself to be the Christ, He proceeds at once to tell His disciples that He must go to Jerusalem and suffer many things of the elders and chief priests and be killed. (He predicts here the Resurrection, but His disciples are too stunned to understand it.)

The same feeling of the necessity of His death is given at the time of arrest. When Peter draws his sword, Jesus tells him to return it to its place. He feels that He can appeal to His Father and receive at once twelve legions of angels. But He adds: "How then should the scriptures be fulfilled, that it must be so?" (Matthew 26:51-54, R.S.V.) This passage also is a tribute to the way in which Jesus interpreted His death as part of the prophetic picture. The necessity for the death of Jesus is given also in the prayer in Gethsemane. At first the prayer is: "My Father, if it be possible, let this cup pass from me; nevertheless, not as I will, but as thou wilt." When He prays the second time He says: "My Father, if this cannot pass unless I drink it, thy will be done." (Matthew 26:39-42, R.S.V.) If we meditate deeply on these passages we must feel that the death of Christ was an essential part of His redemptive work.

Jesus knows that His suffering is vicarious; that is, for others. He says: "The Son of man came . . . to give his life a ransom *for many*." (Matthew 20:28.) The same emphasis on the vicarious nature of His death comes out in the words of institution of the Lord's Supper. Of the bread He says, "This is my body, which is broken *for you.*" (1 Corinthians 11:24.) And as He takes the cup He says, "This is my blood of the new testament, which is shed *for many for the remission of sins.*" (Matthew 26:28.) The last statement shows clearly that in the thought of Jesus the New Covenant was based on His redemptive work. The message of remission of sins comes to us because Christ died for our sins according to the Scriptures. (1 Corinthians 15:3.)

Cleopas had felt that Jesus could not be the Christ because it was not appropriate for the Christ to suffer and die. He learned from the Stranger that Jesus could not have been the Christ apart from the experience of suffering and death. And it was not long before Cleopas learned the identity of the Stranger who walked beside him on the road to Emmaus. As Jesus talked, the hearts of Cleopas and his friend became aflame with a new understanding of the nature of the work of the Christ. The day being far spent, they invited the Stranger to their home. As He blessed the bread, their eyes were opened and they knew they had been in the presence of the living Lord. As they knew Him He vanished from their sight.

Cleopas and his companion hastened to return to Jerusalem. They went as the bearers of good news to the other disciples. They went to add to the story of the empty tomb the account of their contact with the risen Lord. They were met by the disciples, who said to them: "The Lord is risen indeed, and hath appeared to Simon." They arrived in time to be present when the Lord appeared to the disciples, and to hear again His message concerning the necessity for His suffering and death. They received also His commission to proclaim in His name repentance and remission of sins among all nations, beginning at Jerusalem. Cleopas had hoped for One who would redeem Israel. He found One through whom God was reconciling the world unto Himself. He found the "one mediator between God and men, the man Christ Jesus; who gave himself a ransom for all." (1 Timothy 2:5-6.) We can be sure that Cleopas spent the rest of his life in bearing witness to his crucified and risen Lord.

> *"And the Word became flesh, and dwelt among us
> (and we beheld his glory, glory as of the only begot-
> ten from the Father), full of grace and truth."—John
> 1:14,* A.S.V.

> *"We would see Jesus."—John 12:21.*

The Face of the Christ

Scripture background: John 1:1-18; 12:20-50.

During the last week of Jesus' life there were certain
Greeks who came to Philip saying, "Sir, we would see Jesus."
(John 12:21.) These Greeks wanted to see Jesus face to face.
Their desire has been shared by many others. We have not had
preserved for us any authentic description of the physical appearance of Jesus of Nazareth. We do not know whether He was
tall or short, blonde or dark. The stories about Him point to a
man of great physical vitality. His contemporaries likened Him
to Elijah, or to John the Baptist, and the scene in which He
cleanses the Temple suggests a man of commanding strength.
But evidently Jesus' disciples did not think that the details of
His physical appearance were important.

The desire to see Jesus goes much deeper than an interest in
the way He looked. We want to know His character. We want
to know what kind of person He was. When our interest moves
from physical appearance to spiritual qualifications we find that
there has been preserved for us an abundance of material. Jesus
laid upon His disciples the responsibility of being witnesses to
Him. (Acts 1:8.) The apostles clearly understood that their
major responsibility centered in being faithful witnesses to
Jesus Christ. (Acts 2:32; 3:15; 10:39, 41.) The New Testament

comes out of the believing community of the followers of Jesus. It is the written record of the witness of this community to the fact of Jesus Christ.

We have studied in successive chapters the faces of those who stood about the Christ. But these individuals are of abiding significance only because of their relation to the Christ. We have wanted to know what Jesus said to them. We have been interested in their reaction to Him. We have sought to see the face of the Christ in the faces about the Christ. Our purpose now is to gather together these separate reactions in the hope that they will give us a composite picture which will help us to see Him more clearly.

The personalities of the Nativity help us to know that Jesus comes in fulfillment of the whole movement of God in history —a fulfillment to which the Old Testament continually points. Simeon is an old man who has received the promise that he will not see death until he has seen the Lord's Christ. He represents the believing past as it waits for the coming of the Christ. Anna is among those who are looking for the redemption of Jerusalem. The words of Zacharias express his yearning for the coming of the Deliverer of his people. Herod the Great reveals in his brutal slaughter of the innocents his fear of the emergence of a true Son of David whom the people will recognize as the Christ. The note of expectation found in the faces about the manger permeates the whole of the Gospels. When John appears, all men wonder in their hearts whether he is the Christ. (Luke 3:15.) The woman of Samaria speaks for her people as she looks for the coming of the Messiah who will tell them all things.

The Christian Church is founded upon the witness of the apostles to Jesus Christ. The unity of this witness is more important than its diversity. Those who had lived intimately with Jesus in the days of His public ministry stood together as they repeated His teachings, told of His mighty deeds, and gave their united witness to the significance of His death and resurrection. But the New Testament record does give us some of the individual reactions of the members of the band of the apostles. At Caesarea Philippi, Peter is speaking for each of the Twelve as he affirms his belief that Jesus is the Christ, the Son of God. (Matthew 16:16.) He expresses the same basic conviction when in answer to Jesus' question, "Will ye also go away?" he says: "Lord, to whom shall we go? thou hast the words of eternal life. And we believe and are sure that thou art that Christ, the Son of the living God." (John 6:67-69.) In the beginning of Jesus' public ministry, Andrew went out from a conversation with Jesus to find Peter and announce to him, "We have found the Messiah." (John 1:41, R.S.V.) James, the son of Zebedee, stands within the inner circle of the twelve disciples. He is the first of the Twelve to seal his testimony to Jesus with a martyr's death. (Acts 12:2.)

John, the brother of James, comes to belief in the Resurrection as he stands at the empty tomb. The Gospel which bears his name is written that men might believe that Jesus is the Christ, the Son of the living God, and that believing they might have life through His name. (John 20:31.) Jesus finds Philip and says to him, "Follow me." Philip goes from this meeting with Jesus to say to Nathanael: "We have found him, of whom Moses in the law, and the prophets, did write, Jesus of Nazareth, the son of Joseph." (John 1:45.) It is in response to Philip's request for the vision of the Father that Jesus says: "He that hath seen me hath seen the Father." (John 14:9.) Nathanael is so impressed by the supernatural knowledge which Jesus has of him that he says to Jesus: "Rabbi, thou art the Son of God; thou art the King of Israel." (John 1:49.) Jesus replies that this is but the beginning of the signs which Nathanael will see.

Thomas is known as the doubting disciple because of his slowness to believe that Jesus had risen from the dead. But the doubts of Thomas are removed, and he identifies himself with the believing community as he says to Jesus: "My Lord and my God." (John 20:28.) We do not have any specific confession of faith from Matthew, but there is a tradition that Matthew kept a record of the words of Jesus. Matthew's Logia may be the original source of the sayings of Jesus preserved for us in the

Gospel which bears his name. Judas, not Iscariot, does not understand how Jesus can reveal Himself to His disciples and not to the world. He receives from Jesus the statement of knowledge of Him and love and obedience to Him as the spiritual prerequisites for the realization of the sense of the presence of God in Christ. Judas Iscariot will always be known as the disciple who betrayed his Lord. We should remember that Judas in his remorse cries out: "I have sinned in that I have betrayed the innocent blood." (Matthew 27:4.)

Jesus loved the Twelve. He devoted a considerable portion of His ministry to the training of this chosen band of disciples. Some of His most intimate sayings were spoken in the first instance as part of the preparation of the apostles for their responsibility of witnessing to Him. He called them His friends. The condition of continuing in His friendship was obedience to His commands. He called them friends also because He had made known to this chosen group all that He had heard from His Father. (John 15:15.) Jesus loved these disciples with a depth of love which we cannot easily understand. He Himself compares His love for them to the love which He has received from the Father. (John 15:9.) Again He says that the deepest measure of love that we have is the willingness of a man to lay down his life for his friends. He was ready to go to the final limit of devotion. John tells us that Jesus, having loved His own, loved them to the end. (John 13:1.) And as the disciples looked back to their days with Jesus they thought of Him as the one who loved them and gave Himself for them. (Galatians 2:20.)

Jesus was deeply concerned that His disciples should love each other with the love which He had given them. And John feels that the disciples' love for others is rooted in their response to the love of Jesus. (1 John 4:19, A.S.V.)

The apostles' witness to Jesus lays the foundation for the thought and life of the Christian Church, but the record of this witness which we have in the New Testament preserves for us the reactions of Jesus' contemporaries to Him. These reactions are varied. Some of them are from those who became His disci-

ples. Other expressions concerning Him are from those who refused to acknowledge His claims.

Some of the responses to Jesus on the part of those who had
somewhat incidental contacts with Him reveal a remarkable
faith in Him. A Roman centurion believes that Jesus can heal
his servant without coming to see him. Jesus commends his faith
and heals his servant. (Matthew 8:1-13.) The centurion who
executes the sentence of crucifixion comes first to the conviction
that Jesus is a righteous man and then to the belief that He is the
Son of God. (Mark 15:39.) And the dying thief on the cross
has enough confidence in Jesus to ask to be remembered by Him
when He comes into His Kingdom. (Luke 23:42.)

It is particularly interesting to notice the reactions of the
women of the New Testament to Jesus. Mary His mother is
found at the cross and with the believing community in Acts.
(John 19:25; Acts 1:14.) Elisabeth recognizes Mary as the
mother of her Lord. (Luke 1:43.) Anna speaks of Him to all
that look for the redemption of Jerusalem. (Luke 2:38.) A band
of women follow Jesus and minister to Him and His disciples.
These women are found at the cross and at the sepulcher on the
morning of the Resurrection. Jesus appears first to Mary Magdalene. Mary of Bethany loves Jesus with a love that does not
count the cost. Her anointing of Him is told of her wherever
the Gospel is preached. Martha, her sister, responds to His affirmation concerning the resurrection and His question, "Believest
thou this?" by saying, "Yea, Lord: I believe that thou art the
Christ, the Son of God, which should come into the world."
(John 11:26-27.) Jesus dealt tenderly with the women who
came to Him. When the woman who had been a sinner appears
in the home of Simon the Pharisee, Jesus says: "Her sins, which
are many, are forgiven; for she loved much." (Luke 7:47.) And
His gentle consideration for the feelings of the woman taken in
adultery contrasts strongly with the attitude of the Pharisees.
(John 8:3-11.) We need not be surprised to learn that women of
all ages have felt drawn to Jesus of Nazareth.

The references to children in the Gospel narratives are more or less incidental, but they are sufficient to show the love of children which was in the heart of Jesus. He observed the children playing in the market place and used their play to illustrate the inconsistency of the Pharisees in their criticisms of Him and of John the Baptist. (Luke 7:32-34.) When Jesus wanted to teach His disciples about greatness in the Kingdom of heaven, He called a little child and set him in the midst of them. In the discourse which follows we feel His love for children. He identifies Himself with children everywhere when He says, "Whoso shall receive one such little child in my name receiveth me." (Matthew 18:5.) Jesus is so completely identified with little children that the things we do for them are accepted as our ministry to Him. In Matthew 18:6 we feel the full force of His wrath against anyone who would harm a little child. In this setting we can understand His rebuke of His disciples when they sought to prevent the mothers from bringing their children to Him for Him to bless them. We must not forget that Jesus said of children: "Suffer little children, and forbid them not, to come unto me: for of such is the kingdom of heaven." (Matthew 19:14.) One of the bright spots in the tragic events of the last week is the scene in which the children in the Temple are crying, "Hosanna to the son of David." (Matthew 21:15.)

While the leaders of the Jews were cautious in their response to Jesus, the common people heard Him gladly. (Mark 12:37.) Part of His popularity was undoubtedly due to His ministry of healing. The people flocked to Him to be healed of their diseases. Another source of His popularity was His manner of teaching. He knew how to paint pictures and tell stories, and He taught with a note of authority which contrasted strangely with the teaching of the scribes. (Mark 1:22.) It is true that the chief priests and elders persuaded the Jerusalem mob to ask for the crucifixion of Jesus, but throughout His ministry as a whole the people were on His side. Most of them must have understood His compassion as He looked out upon the multitude. Jesus was concerned for the physical well-being of the people. Before He performed the miracle of feeding the four thousand He said: "I have compassion on the multitude, because they continue with me now three days, and have nothing to eat: and I will not send them away fasting, lest they faint in the way." (Matthew 15:32.) But deeper than His concern for the hunger of their bodies was His compassion on the spiritual need of the unshepherded multitude. "When he saw the multitudes, he was moved with compassion on them, because they fainted, and were scattered abroad, as sheep having no shepherd." (Matthew 9:36.) Jesus' attitude toward the multitude contrasts strongly with the scorn of the Pharisees. When the soldiers sent to arrest Jesus returned without Him, saying, "Never man spake like this man," the Pharisees replied: "Are ye also deceived? Have any of the rulers or of the Pharisees believed on him? But this people who knoweth not the law are cursed." (John 7:46-49.) The appeal of Jesus to the common people served for a time to hold in check the determination of the Jewish leaders to destroy Him.

Our record of the attitude of those who opposed Jesus has come to us through His disciples. But we do not need to doubt the accuracy of their reports, and from them we can draw a picture of the various reactions to Jesus which were found in the ranks of those who did not follow Him. The center of the opposition to Jesus during most of His public ministry was to be found with the Pharisees. In the beginning there may have been some effort on their part to find a common ground with Him. Nicodemus was a Pharisee. He had evidently discussed with some of his friends the mighty works of the Prophet from Nazareth. They had reached the conclusion that Jesus must be a teacher sent from God. They did not see how any man could do the works that Jesus did unless God was with Him. But the approach of Nicodemus failed. Neither Nicodemus nor his friends were willing to make the kind of surrender that Jesus demanded. Jesus' being invited to the home of Simon the Pharisee may have been another attempt of the Pharisees to come to terms with Him. Simon was critical, but he did invite Jesus to his home. The beginning of offense with the Pharisees was probably Jesus' claim to have power on earth to forgive sins.

The Pharisees saw the implications of this claim and were shocked by it. As soon as the line of division had been drawn, they found other points of disagreement. Jesus did not observe the Sabbath day in the manner prescribed by the Pharisees. They were outraged by His attitude toward the publicans and the harlots. The Pharisees did not approve when Jesus chose Matthew, a publican, to be a member of His band of disciples. They were offended when Jesus and His disciples attended a banquet given by Matthew. Jesus Himself says that the Pharisees say of Him: "Behold a man gluttonous, and a winebibber, a friend of publicans and sinners." (Matthew 11:19.) The first two terms are obviously the exaggeration of an enemy. They do reveal Jesus as a man who has in Him nothing of the ascetic. He was not ashamed to enjoy eating and drinking. But we cannot think of Him as a glutton or a drunkard. In its original setting, the phrase, "friend of publicans," was intended as an insult. The Pharisees were shocked at the way Jesus defied the established lines of caste.

The Pharisees faced the necessity of attempting to explain the works of Jesus. They could not acknowledge that He was a teacher sent from God without being embarrassed when they were asked why they had not accepted His teachings. They suggested therefore that Jesus cast out devils by being in league with Beelzebub, the prince of the devils. Jesus was quick to tell them that the suggestion did not make sense. Jesus was obviously in conflict with the kingdom of evil. The moral enormity of the sin of attributing the works of Jesus of Nazareth to the power of Satan reveals the desperation of the Pharisees as they sought to explain the works of Jesus. (Matthew 12:24-32.)

The full depth of the conflict between Jesus and the Pharisees is set forth in the familiar twenty-third chapter of Matthew. His basic charge against them is that of hypocrisy. The Pharisees are acting a part. They are making professions which they are not translating into life. They do their works to be seen of men. Their righteousness is that of external conformity to a code. Behind their pious front they are full of hypocrisy and iniquity. We need to heed Jesus' words to the Pharisees because the sins of the Pharisees are the sins into which respectable people fall when they forget that their salvation is by grace alone.

With rare irony Jesus accused the Pharisees of building the tombs of the prophets and garnishing the sepulchers of the righteous while they themselves were seeking to destroy the One whom God had sent to them. It is still more popular to honor dead prophets than to listen to living ones. The indictment which Jesus made of the Pharisees was deep and searching. We can understand why they were convinced that the Prophet from Nazareth must be silenced. But the wrath of Jesus against the Pharisees roots in His love for them. The invective of the indictment is followed by the lament over Jerusalem as she kills the prophets and stones those that are sent unto her. Of this Jerusalem, Jesus says: "How often would I have gathered thy children together, even as a hen gathereth her chickens under her wings, and ye would not!" (Matthew 23:37.)

Jesus also faced the Sadducees. They were the cynics of the time. If the leaven of the Pharisees was insincerity, the leaven of the Sadducees was unbelief. The Sadducees professed faith in the God of Israel, and they were loyal to the letter of the law. In the beginning their refusal to accept the hope of the resurrection of the dead was grounded in their failure to find it in their Scriptures. In its practical outworking, the unbelief of the Sadducees resulted in the rejection of the hope of life after death and in the denial of the reality of the whole spirit world. Jesus warns against the leaven of the Sadducees, but He does not come into conflict with them very frequently. The Sadducees do come to Him during Passion Week with a stock illustration in which they attempt to ridicule the doctrine of the resurrection of the dead. Jesus says that they have failed to understand their Scriptures or to appreciate the power of God. He insists that they are wrong in their denial of the hope of the resurrection. The Sadducees have little in common with the Pharisees, but they join them in the conviction that Jesus must be destroyed. (Matthew 22:23-33; Mark 12:18-27; Luke 20:27-38.)

The real conflict of Jesus with the Sadducees centered in the opposition of the chief priests. The priests belonged to the party of the Sadducees. Their attitude is expressed in the consultation held after they had received the report of the raising of Lazarus. They say: "What do we? for this man doeth many miracles. If we let him thus alone, all men will believe on him: and the Romans shall come and take away both our place and nation." (John 11:47-48.) The priests are forced to admit the mighty works of Jesus. They do not seriously wrestle with the implications of these miracles, but they are concerned lest Jesus become the leader of a Messianic revolt which might result in the destruction of the Jewish nation. In this situation Caiaphas speaks for them when he insists that it is better for one man to die than for the whole nation to perish. The priests' opposition to Jesus was probably intensified by His attack on entrenched graft in His cleansing of the Temple, but they were seeking to bring about His death before this incident took place. It is fair to say that the chief priests along with the Pharisees were shocked by the implications of the claims of Jesus. In the trial before Caiaphas, Jesus is condemned as guilty of blasphemy. Toward the end of the trial before Pilate, Jesus' accusers are forced to say: "We have a law, and by our law he ought to die, because he made himself the Son of God." (John 19:7.) And when Jesus is on the cross the chief priests mock Him by saying that He who saved others is now unable to save Himself and by reminding Him of His claim to be the Son of God. (Matthew 27:42-43.)

It was not until the end of His ministry that Jesus came into actual conflict with the rulers of Galilee and Judea. But much of His public ministry was carried on in the territory ruled by Herod Antipas. He heard of the fame of Jesus, and, like the rest of his contemporaries, found it necessary to offer some explanation of the mighty works of Jesus. He said to his servants: "This is John the Baptist; he is risen from the dead; and therefore mighty works do shew forth themselves in him." (Matthew 14:2.) Herod's explanation was probably not very satisfying either to him or to his servants. It does point up the way in which even Herod had to seek to explain the unique figure of

THE FACE OF THE CHRIST

Jesus. Pilate faces Jesus as a Roman who is not completely familiar with the religious life of the Jews. He is soon convinced of Jesus' innocence of any crimes which are a threat to the Roman state. But Pilate, too, is gradually seized with a sense of dread as he faces the person of Jesus. This feeling is probably intensified by the message from his wife and by the Jews' statement that Jesus had claimed to be the Son of God. The final scene in which Pilate washes his hands to rid himself of the sense of guilt in condemning Jesus is an indication of the impact of Jesus on the Roman governor.

We have sought to see the face of the Christ in the reactions of His friends and His enemies. The time has now come to draw some conclusions which have grown out of the witness to Him in the New Testament as a whole. The Jesus who meets us here is fully human. He is born of a woman. We see Him as a baby in His mother's arms. We have a glimpse of Him as a boy of twelve making the trip from Nazareth to Jerusalem. He is known as the carpenter of Nazareth. The people of Nazareth know of His mother and His brothers and sisters. He experiences hunger and thirst and weariness. He loves Mary and Martha and Lazarus. He enters into the experience of temptation. He is grateful to His disciples because they have continued with Him in His temptations. (Luke 22:28.) He dies on a Roman cross. His body is buried in the tomb of Joseph of Arimathaea. We do not have here a theophany in which God appears in the form of a man. We have instead the life of a man who appears at a definite time and place in human history and enters into the total range of our human experience.

But the witness to Jesus is clear in its insistence that He exercised among us powers that were more than human. There was about Him from the beginning something that marked Him as different from those around Him. He speaks always with the note of authority. In the beginning of His ministry he puts forth in veiled form the claim to have power on earth to forgive sins. He supports this claim with a miracle of healing. (Mark 2:1-12.) He claims to be Lord of the Sabbath. (Mark 2:23-28.) He commands the winds and the waves. His disciples, marveling, say: "What manner of man is this, that even the wind and the sea obey him?" (Mark 4:41.) He raises the daughter of Jairus (Mark 5:35-43) and multiplies the loaves and the fishes (Mark 6:31-45). He sends the disciples of John the Baptist back to him with the message: "Go and shew John again those things which ye do hear and see: The blind receive their sight, and the lame walk, the lepers are cleansed, and the deaf hear, the dead are raised up, and the poor have the gospel preached to them. And blessed is he, whosoever shall not be offended in me." (Matthew 11:4-6.) Jesus rises from the dead on the third day. He sends His followers to make disciples of all nations and to teach them to observe the things which He has commanded, promising to be with them to the end of the age. (Matthew 28:19-20.) He ascends up into heaven and pours out His Spirit on His followers. We may properly raise some questions about the details of some of the deeds attributed to Jesus of Nazareth, but to attempt to eliminate completely the supernatural element in the record is to destroy the basic integrity of the witness of the New Testament to Jesus. Both His friends and His foes admitted that there was something out of the ordinary about Jesus which needed explanation. The difference was in the way they sought to explain Him.

As we study the face of the Christ we are impressed by the absolute nature of His claims. He describes Himself as meek and lowly in heart, but He does this as part of the statement in which He invites all who labor and are heavy-laden to come to Him that they may find rest for their souls. (Matthew 11:28-30.) He teaches the disciples humility by washing their feet, but He does this in the knowledge that He has come from God and goes to God. And after He has completed this task of a servant He says to His disciples: "Ye call me Master and Lord: and ye say well; for so I am." (John 13:13.) The understanding of *who He is* is implicit in many of the actions of Jesus; it underlies all that He says and does. But it becomes explicit in some statements. He claims to have power on earth to forgive sins, and He does not alter this claim when the Pharisees reason in their hearts: "Why doth this man thus speak blasphemies? who can forgive sins but God only?" (Mark 2:7.) When the woman of Samaria refers to the coming of the Christ, Jesus says to her: "I that speak unto thee am he." (John 4:26.) Consider in this connection the great *I am* statements of Jesus. "I am that bread of life." (John 6:48.) "I am the light of the world." (John 8:12.) "I am the good shepherd." (John 10:14.) "I am the way, the truth, and the life." (John 14:6.) And He says to Philip: "He that hath seen me hath seen the Father." (John 14:9.)

The seeming arrogance of Jesus' claims is matched by the imperious nature of His demands on men. He asked of men a loyalty which was complete and final. He says: "If any man come to me, and hate not his father, and mother, and wife, and children, and brethren, and sisters, yea, and his own life also, he cannot be my disciple." (Luke 14:26.) We know that Jesus does not mean this to be taken literally. He does not teach us to hate. But the verse does express the way in which the call of Jesus must take precedence over all the lesser loyalties of life. He insists that before men start to follow Him they should count the cost. The cost is high because Jesus has said, "Whosoever he be of you that forsaketh not all that he hath, he cannot be my disciple." (Luke 14:33.) Who is this Person who dares to make this kind of demand upon His followers?

The demands of Jesus are balanced by His promises. He tells His disciples that in His death He is going to prepare a place for them and that He will come again and receive them unto Himself. (John 14:3.) After the conversation with the rich young ruler He promises the disciples who have left all to follow Him the deepest satisfactions of this life and, in the world to come, eternal life. (Luke 18:29-30.) He tells the thief on the cross that he will pass through death to paradise. (Luke 23:43.) And as He looks forward to His death by crucifixion He says: "And I, if I be lifted up from the earth, will draw all men unto me." (John 12:32.)

All of those who came into serious contact with Jesus felt the unique nature of the man with whom they were dealing. In this His friends and foes were agreed. The enemies of Jesus made various inadequate efforts to account for Him. They were left finally with the great enigma. They were attempting to explain a Person who could not be fully understood on their premises. And as the Gospel narratives draw to a close we become increasingly conscious of the blindness which is falling on those who are opposed to Jesus. Jesus weeps over Jerusalem as He says: "If thou hadst known, even thou, at least in this thy day, the things which belong unto thy peace! but now they are hid from thine eyes." (Luke 19:42.) His tears flow also because He knows that the way of rejection and of blindness leads inevitably to judgment.

The followers of Jesus felt that the only adequate explanation of Him was the acknowledgment of the truth of His claims and the surrender to Him as Lord and Saviour. The crucial fact in their thinking was the Resurrection. Peter could say to the Jerusalem mob: "This Jesus hath God raised up, whereof we all are witnesses. . . . Therefore let all the house of Israel know assuredly, that God hath made that same Jesus, whom ye have crucified, both Lord and Christ." (Acts 2:32, 36.) And Paul could write: "Concerning his Son Jesus Christ our Lord . . . declared to be the Son of God with power . . . by the resurrection from the dead." (Romans 1:3-4.)

The writers of the New Testament were sure that Jesus of Nazareth was the risen Lord. This conviction had implications for their understanding of the life of Jesus. Those who had come to believe in Him as the risen Lord, forever present with His Church, went back to their memories of Him in the days of His flesh. They saw the events of His life in a dimension of depth which could not have been fully present with them when these events were taking place. Every detail of the Church's memory of her Lord became significant in the light of the faith of the Church in His resurrection and exaltation. And the memory of the life of Jesus gave abiding content to the worship of the Christian community. The worship of the first Christians was directed to the God who had come to them in Jesus Christ. But these Christians never forgot that their knowledge of the character of God and of His will for them was rooted in the Christ event. They looked to the life, death, and resurrection of Jesus as the point at which God had made Himself known. The content of their worship of the eternal God was rooted in their memory of the face of the Christ. The early Christians were sure that "God was in Christ, reconciling the world unto himself." (2 Corinthians 5:19.) They were confident that when they had seen the face of the Christ they had seen also the face of the Father who had sent Him. They knew that they had seen the "light of the knowledge of the glory of God in the face of Jesus Christ." (2 Corinthians 4:6.) Those who saw beyond the veil of flesh to the vision of the face of the Christ knew that they had seen a face of inexpressible loveliness. They knew also that they must respond to Him in love and obedience.